"WHOA MAN!"

SEE WHAT GOD DID WITH A RIB!

PAT MALLORY

PRESS

TABLE OF CONTENTS

INTRODUCTION

There is a joke going around that goes something like this: God made man and realized he was flawed so SHE created woman...and so the battle of the sexes continues. A battle that is, in and of itself, contrary to the will of God. When God created mankind, He included two equal parts, male and female. God's perfect plan was that these two equal beings would function as one in having dominion over the earth, in procreation and in fellowship with God. Woman was not an afterthought, but rather an important part of God's plan from the beginning.

The differences in the materials used in their respective creations does not make either superior or inferior, but rather points to differences in each one's function especially in procreation. Man was made from dust and woman was taken from man and formed from his rib, but just as man is not subject to the dust from which he was formed, neither is woman subject to man's rib nor man from which she was formed. God was the creator not the materials He used. God alone has dominion over mankind. I Corinthians 11:12 states that "For as woman came from man, so also man is born of woman. BUT everything comes from God." In the first chapter of Genesis beginning with the twenty-sixth verse we read that "In the beginning"—God said: "Let us make man in our own image"—So God created man in His own image, in the image of God created He him; male and female created He them." Mary J. Evans, in her book "Women in the Bible", points out that God is neither male nor female since God does not have a physical body. Therefore the phrase "in our own image" does not relate to our physical make-up, but rather to our nature and moral images. Our nature was created in God's image so that we can think, reason and have a will. Our moral image was created in God's image so that we originally shared in His goodness.

In all of God's instruction to His creation, He gave equal dominion and responsibility to both male and female. After the fall of both man and woman in the Garden of Eden, both were held accountable only to God. Both man and woman were judged and punished by God for their individual actions. But, even then, we see Adam recognizing the worth of woman in God's plan. He names her Eve and called her the "Mother of all living".

A search through scripture reveals that God's will for women was always one of equality with man, the one exception being in marriage. In marriage the woman is to be submissive to the man as a matter of choice and in respect for God's wisdom. The term sub-mission means that man and woman are together on a mission in this world but when they come to an impasse if is God's plan that the woman voluntarily yield her will to man. This is necessary because as a path narrows there is only room for one point man, so to speak, and God directs that the point man, in the context of marriage, be the male part of His creation. This does not mean that woman cannot point out pitfalls or different pathways, but when decision time comes and there is not agreement then the woman submits her will to that of man. Nor does it necessarily follow that man has superior knowledge, but rather man is designed by God to head up the team. The term "woman" is used 352 times in scripture and nowhere is the admonition "to be obedient" used in the male-female relationship. Also there is always the qualification that man is to love and care for the woman as Christ loved the Church. Sub-mission is easy in an atmosphere of love. God did not intend for woman to be a slave nor a doormat. In Romans 7:2 we see where woman is released from this submission outside of marriage. It reads: for the woman which had a husband is bound by the law to her husband so long as he liveth; but if the husband be dead, she is loosed from the law of her husband." The Apostle Paul's admonitions concerning women are to be viewed in light of the context in which they were written. Paul was writing letters to specific churches concerning specific problems within their fellowship and particular society which need to be considered in understanding and interpreting Paul's writings.

Patriarch societies have seized upon God's plan and in many instances subverted God's intent for a myriad of reasons...fear and a desire for control paramount among them. Man has given woman inferior places in society, but this is not by God's will, design, sanction nor practice. From Genesis to Revelation we see God treating men and women as equals in all areas including the law. Adam recognized that Eve was like him when he stated "This is bone of my bone and flesh of my flesh." Eve certainly did not have to ask Adam's permission before she dealt with the serpent and ate of the fruit of the tree, although, in retrospect, it might have been a good idea. A quick read through of God's law in the Old Testament reveals, in every instance, the laws apply equally to man and woman. They are equal in ability to approach God directly through prayer, praise and worship. Women are given tasks to perform for God. They are told to be witnesses, teachers, judges and prophets. Scripture reveals astute money managers, business women, believers, deaconesses, disciples, leaders and skilled workers among its women. They are judged, reprimanded, touched, forgiven and commissioned. Women are considered as wise counselors, fellow-laborers in Christ Jesus and worthy to participate in discussions and debates concerning spiritual matters. They are to be respected and have rights.

Jesus trusted women with important details of His ministry. He counted them among His closest friends and followers. He commended them for their faithfulness and discernment. God chose a woman to bring His only Son into the world and when Jesus rose from the grave His first appearance was to a woman. One of Jesus' last statements on the cross was to a woman, His mother, and about a woman, also His mother. The women o remained loyal until the end. Women were the last to leave the cross, the first to believe He had risen from the grave and they were the first to share the good news with others.

There are over 300 engaging and insightful portraits of women in the Bible: 188 are names; 144, unnamed. There are 40 daughters of, 28 wives of, 24 mothers of, 8 widows of, 1 grandmother of and 44 others. These women in the Bible are of all ages. They are married, divorced, never-married and widowed. They are good, bad and indifferent. They are queens, servants, mothers, grandmothers, daughters, nieces, sisters, aunts. There are women of prominence and those who remain in the background. Marital status was not a criteria for being used by God. They, as women today, were all in need of a Savior. So God sent His only begotten Son so that WHOSOEVER believeth in Him might be saved. Saved to serve, worship, praise and share the gospel with the lost. Saved to encourage and help others along the way, until that day when Jesus comes again to take His creation home again.

The following profiles in the Bible are portraits of what God did with a rib. Look at them and then pull out your mirror and take a good look at yourself because you too are a special creation, unique and needed in the kingdom of God. Created by God in His own image.

WOMEN IN THE BEGINNING

CREATION, LIGHT, LIFE, A GARDEN,

the fall, A FAMILY, the flood,

A DOVE, A RAINBOW, AN ALTAR,

a falling tower, a scattering,

A COVENANT, A JOURNEY, A HOME, A TIME OF
PLENTY,

disobedience, a time of famine, captivity.

"Up and down and all around"; this could be the theme song of the beginning. There would be a drawing close to God followed by a slipping away. This seemed to be the cycle of life, yet, through it all, God raised up some notable women. Women whose lives have a message for women today as we strive to serve our Redeemer; knowing that, because of Him, we can never slip away again. We may fall down, but because He holds us in His Hands we know that we are secure forever.

These are the women of the beginning—.first, there was Eve.

Gen. 2:19-4:26

EVE (life)

"Mother of all living", she was called,
This first woman named Eve.
Life was perfect - she had it all,
Until she was deceived.

The serpent planted a doubt,
Then implied God had lied.
Eve went to check it out;
She would not be denied.

Um— It tasted so good!
And hey, now she could see
This was much more than food,
Why, this tree was a key.

A key to unlock the door
And give her entrance in
To all God had in store
From the beginning to the end.

Eve could hardly wait
Once she had a bite
To share with her mate
This tasty gourmet delight.

But the sweet became bitter
And much, much too soon.
Summer turned into winter
And dark became the moon.

Now from the Garden she must go
To suffer pain upon the earth.
Her punishment while here below
Would be felt as she gave birth.

But greater far than physical pain
Was the pain within her heart.
Pain that was hard to explain,
Because all had turned so very dark.

For the issue from her loins
Were fraught with evil deeds.
'Twas the "reward" for one who joined
Satan, and signed his evil creed.

No longer were all things well,
It could never be the same,
For now when night time fell,
God no longer came.

LESSONS FROM EVE

Eve was the final act of God in creation. She was equal to the male part in every way. In fact, man was not given dominion over the animals and the earth until woman was standing by his side. She had a free will and the right of choice. It is her choices and the consequences of those choices for which she is most remembered. She chose to believe the lies of Satan rather than the truths of God. She chose to involve Adam in those choices. Eve then had to face the judgment of God for those choices and pay the price for disobedience to God. She also had to live with the resulting consequences.

Women today are also free agents and have the right to make choices. We need to remember that, like Eve, we also will have to face judgment and pay a price for disobedience to God. We have to live with the consequences of those choices. If we would look back over our lives we could trace every situation we find ourselves in back to a choice we have made. This should tell us to be very careful in our choices.

But even more serious is the fact that we are not the only ones who pay for the choices we make. Good and bad choices in life have a ripple effect upon those around us, particularly those we love. We need to consider very carefully the choices that come our way. Are they in line with God's will? What is our motive? Will they be as appealing tomorrow? What harm can they cause in my life and the lives of others? How dark will be the night when we separate ourselves from God?

God's forgiveness can also be seen in the life of Eve. All of the great epochs in a woman's life, her marriage, mating and motherhood unfold in all of their completeness in the Genesis account of Eve. Though Eve fell far short of the ideal in womanhood, she rose to the dream of her destiny as a wife and mother. Paradise had been lost, but something wonderful, maternal care had been born. In Eve, motherhood became a great sacrifice and a sublime service. Because of her children, Eve knew that God was still in this universe which He had created. She was to see the fulfillment of God's plan in her own life. Cain married and Eve had a grandchild, Enoch as well as other heirs. It was through her son Seth that the ancestry of Jesus Christ can be traced. So take heart women of today, even if you should slip and fall into temptations snares, God can and will give you a second chance and make you useful in His Kingdom if you, but turn to Him.

Gen. 11-25

SARAH (princess)

Sarah was Abraham's wife.
Her beauty was renowned.
She was the love of his life,
This truth in scripture is found.

They married in the land of Ur,
The traveled at God's command.
When others had a desire for her,
A lie became their stand.

But, alas she had no son,
So Sarah took control.
She found another one,
To give Abraham console.

This plan backfired on her,
And much to her regret.
Sarah caused quite a stir
As she began to fret.

God said He would send a son:
But this made Sarah laugh,
Until the deed was truly done
And God intervened on her behalf.

Sarah was ninety on the day
Isaac became her son.
Now she trusted in God's way
From that day on—

LESSONS FROM SARAH

Sarah was the wife of Abraham. God had chosen Abraham to be the father of a great nation. This meant that Sarah was to be the mother of a great nation. What a special privilege! But Sarah was getting impatient. She and Abraham had traveled far from their home, faced many perils and yet she had no children. How, she must have wondered, could she be the mother of a great nation unless she bore sons? Because of her impatience, Sarah jumped ahead of God and took matters into her own hands. She decided that she would arrange for those sons through a substitute mother, her handmaid Hagar. When this plan went awry and God again told her she would have a son, Sarah laughed at God is disbelief, after all she was no longer the beautiful young maiden, but now an old lady.

Beauty is a very special gift from God, but is not to be misused. True beauty is in a heart that yields itself to the will of God. Just as Sarah discovered that physical beauty can become a burden, women today need to ignore the admonitions of the world that only a size five with perfect hair and features is acceptable.

Sarah also teaches us the importance of waiting upon the Lord and the folly of taking control of our lives. While modern authors would have us believe this is the key to fulfillment, God's word teaches us otherwise. God's timing is perfect and prevents the remorse that comes from moving too soon. We can trust in the God who made us and knows us best. Then our hysterical laughter will turn into joy!

Sarah shared her husband's dangers and heartaches and also his great purposes and dreams. When he built an altar and worshiped God, so did Sarah. The beautiful confidence and true affection existing between Sarah and Abraham are reflected in the authority she had over his household during his absence. Abraham recognized Sarah as his equal. She never subjected herself to a lesser role, and Abraham never demanded it. Sarah was a woman of power, as are women today. We need to seek God's guidance in using this power so that we do not fall into some of the same pitfalls that Sarah encountered.

Sarah is the first woman in the Bible to extend hospitality to guests. These guests turned out to be divine messengers. Could we not learn the importance of hospitality from our sister Sarah? Sarah developed great faith. This can be seen in the type of son she raised. Surely the tenderhearted qualities of Isaac were evidence of the gentle influence of his mother in his formative years. We, as mothers today, need to realize the influence we have over our children. Then, like Sarah, we need to make that influence one that will be pleasing to God. Then God will allow us to have the rights due to women. Sarah is the only woman in the Bible whose age at death is recorded. This signifies the important place she held in the minds of early Hebrews and God.

Gen. 16: 1-16; 21: 1-21

HAGAR (stranger)

Hagar was an Egyptian maid,
Who her mistress betrayed,
After spending just one night
Acting as Abram's wife.

For Sarai had borne no sons,
and hoped for Hagar to bear one.
But when Hagar conceived life,
Sarai was despised in her sight.

So Sarai complained to her man,
Who said, "Hagar's fate is in your hand."
Then Sarai treated Hagar so harshly,
That from her presence she did flee.

T'was by the spring on the way to Shur
The angel of the Lord found her.
He said to go on back home
And give birth to this your son.

"I will multiply your seed,
Of your affliction I take heed."
Ishmael you shall name your child,
For he, like an ass, will be wild.

After fourteen years went by
Hagar was again made to cry.
For god had given Sarah a son,
He was to be the special one.

Although Abraham was greatly depressed,
His wife Sarah would have no less.
So into the wilderness they were led,
With only a skin of water and bread.

Hagar did not want to see her son die,
So she lifted her voice to the sky.
God said "I will make a great nation of him,
Then revealed a well of water to them.

Ishmael, an archer became,
In the wilderness of Paran.
His descendants became the Arab race,
Ever an affront to Israel's face.

LESSONS FROM HAGAR

Hagar was the handmaid of Sarai, who was the wife of Abram. Sarai had no children, so as was the custom of the day, she sent her handmaid into her husband. The idea was for the child that she bore to become the child of Sarai. But Hagar wanted both Abram and their son, Ishmael. This started a continuing battle between these two women for the affections of Abram. Later, when God changed the names of Abram and Sarai to Abraham and Sarah, He promised them a son. When this son, Isaac, was born, his mother, Sarah, wanted Hagar and Ishmael to be disinherited. To please Sarah, Abraham sent them away. God heard Hagar's cry for mercy and intervened on her behalf even though He knew that Hagar would ultimately go back to serving her idols. Because of Hagar and Ishmael's choice to assert themselves rather than to live by faith in Abraham's God, the history of the world has been affected.

We can learn from Hagar to look to God for our salvation and our sustenance.

We can learn to remember the times when God has rescued us in life's situations so that our faith grows.

We can learn the results of trying to take matters into our own hands.

Hagar is evidence to each of us that in spite of everything, God loves people.

When we turn to Him, He is always there.

But He is also faithful to keep His promises to us. This applies equally to judgment and grace.

God has a plan for each of our lives.

Our part is to trust in God and His ways so that He can accomplish His plan in the way that is most beneficial to each of us.

Always remember, God knows best.

Gen. 24-49

REBEKAH (enchanting beauty)

Rebekah was a woman of action.
She always took the lead.
It gave her great satisfaction
To meet each and every need.

T'was this trait of hers,
Upon one day at a well,
That caught the eye of Elizer
And put him in her spell.

For he was looking for a wife,
T'was the reason he had come,
To complete Isaac's life
And give him many sons.

So Rebekah agreed to go
And became Isaac's wife.
Then very soon she showed
Inside of her was a new life.

She gave birth to twin boys,
But her love dwelt upon one.
Divided homes bring no joy,
Soon a deceptive plot was spun.

Rebekah deceived her man
And also betrayed a son.
A mistake in her plan,
Yet—the deed was done.

Actions and deeds can be good
When they fit into God's plan.
But it must be understood
Only the just will stand.

LESSONS FROM REBEKAH

To be a woman of action can be a good thing if we consult God before we act.

It would save us monumental grief if we would learn to stop, look and listen for a word from God before we leap into situations that are sometimes beyond our capabilities.

If there is ever an example as to why God wanted woman to be submissive within marriage Rebekah is it.

Rebekah was chaste,

courteous,

helpful,

industrious

and trusting.

She was a woman of sympathy, foresight and religious fervor. She enjoyed peace at home - a good marriage. She had the first monogamous marriage on record. She became so self -serving that lying became a way of life for her. Her example also led her children down a destructive path.

Once action has been taken or words spoken they can never be taken back, nor the resulting consequences. Women need to be a cohesive force within their families not the sword that cuts the family apart. God's plan was for women to work within the family structure. Marriage was God' perfect plan for His creation, but we also need to be aware that, after the fall, we live in a world of darkness where Satan is allowed to set his traps. There are no perfect marriages except the marriage of Christ to His Church. But this does not mean that we as women are not to do our very best to keep the home fires glowing with a loving and gentle spirit when this is possible. Circumstances in today's world, however, sometimes leave women as the head of their families, but we need to give that headship back to God.

Rebekah perhaps typifies the mother down through the ages who, weak in faith, imagines herself to be carrying out the will of God. Rebekah was not willing to assume all the responsibility for her deception. The result, for Rebekah, was grief, which is the same result that will come for women today who allow their fears to overwhelm them and make them forget the part God has in the affairs of men, Rebekah lost the respect of her husband, suffered the anger of one son, and the loss of another. She never saw Jacob, her favorite son again. Ladies, beware, the price may be more than you are willing to pay just to gain your way.

Gen. 29-35:20

RACHEL (an ewe)

Rachel was the object of—
Jacob's undying love.
He found her at a well;
All others began to pale.

He worked seven years for her,
Not once did his love blur;
Tricked upon his wedding nite;
Sister Leah became his wife.

But, Jacob's love was strong,
His heart to Rachel belonged.
So he worked seven years more;
Considered it not even a chore.

But, Rachel never quite knew
About this love so good and true.
She thought that her worth
Rested upon a son's birth.

True love is never earned;
A lesson to be learned.
This truth not to know
Brings sorrow while here below.

After many barren years,
Two sons did appear.
Joseph and Benjamin came
According to God's plan.

Many sorrows and tearful days
Hurt and hindered the way
Of a life filled with love
And blessed by God above.

LESSONS FROM RACHEL

Can you imagine the problems that arose in this polygamous household, where two sisters were married to the same man? Rachel who was introduced as graceful, gentle and lovely became petulant, peevish and self-willed as she was overwhelmed with jealousy of her sister and the children she bore.

Why, oh why is it so hard for women to recognize that they are acceptable. Acceptable not because of what they do, how they look, their age, education, or station in life. Acceptance that says if, when or because is not acceptance at all. God says "I have made you with loving-kindness" and He says that nothing can separate us from the love of God. Yet, like Rachel, we too often feel our acceptance is performance oriented. True, this attitude is touted by society, but is totally contrary to the truth according to God who is the author of truth.

Women can also learn from Rachel that God's timing is perfect! Never despair because the best is yet to come. When one is a child of God, He knows the way so we can rest in that knowledge with confidence that God is in His heaven and all is right with the world, even though that is not what the six o'clock news would have us believe.

Dry your tears and let go of your fears because God says that His joy is yours in this moment. Joy that is not dependent upon circumstances, but upon the one and only God who is all knowing, all- powerful and everywhere! Open up your heart today.

Rachel and Leah regarded themselves, as did their husband Jacob, as their husband's equal. When times of decision came Jacob did not make the decisions alone. He consulted his wives, in fact, he took no major steps without counseling his wives. Rachel's council was not always wise. She had brought with her from her father's household idols that were worshiped by her father. Why? Possibly, Rachel stole them from her father's home to insure the future prosperity of her husband, possibly they were a good luck charm for her, regardless, they caused her to lie to both her husband and her father. As the idols were later buried we can believe that Rachel learned to trust and believe in the God of Jacob.

The lesson we need to learn from this experience of Rachel's is to trust in the one true God from the beginning and understand the consequences of even the smallest lie.

Remember, God's Word tell us to "be sure, your sins will find you out."

Gen. 38:6-30

TAMAR (palm tree)

Tamar was once a blushing bride;
Chosen to walk by Er's side.
Now Er was Judah's oldest son,
As Judah was Jacob's first one.

Tamar thought she wed a godly man,
But alas he was full of evil plans.
His deeds so angered God,
He took Er from earth's sod.

So now according to the law,
Tamar looked to her father-in-law.
Judah turned to his son, Onan,
Stating he should take her hand.

All the children that she bore
Would then Er's name restore.
Onan obeyed, but insulted his wife,
For this, God also took his life.

Now Judah looked on Tamar as a curse,
Ignored God's law; put himself first.
For he did not want to lose again,
A third son when he became a man.

Tamar soon began to realize,
Judah thought her not a prize,
So she took her fate in her hand,
To set things right was her plan.

Tamar tricked Judah in his grief,
Came in the night like a thief.
Judah gave up his staff, cord and seal,
To seal the bargain and their deal.

Abused and neglected was this woman,
Yet God allowed her to bear two men.
When we trace the thread of Christ,
Of only five women, Tamar is first.

LESSONS FROM TAMAR

Tamar lived in a time when the laws of the tribe to which she now belonged, due to her marriage to Er, prohibited a childless woman from remaining a widow.

It was believed that the name of a man could not, under any circumstances, go into oblivion.

It was customary for a man's brother to take his brother's widow as his wife and for her children to be the heirs of the dead brother.

It is easy to see why this system was rife with problems.

Judah, after losing two sons, was not excited about giving another one to Tamar so he put her off until his third son was grown. Tamara went back to her parents' house. As time went by, it became obvious that Judah had gone back on his deal. Tamar decided to take matters in her own hands. She fooled Judah into thinking that she was a temple prostitute. He went in to her and later when he realized that she was with child, he demanded her death. Tamar faced him with his seal and staff. Judah realized that his was the greater sin.

For he had not only sinned against Tamar, but against God.

Tamar was vindicated and given her rightful place.

This teaches us that while God does not approve of sin, He can and does work His plans even through our failings.

Tamar's experience shows the depth of God's love.

God is not afraid to identify with all. God wants women to have their rightful position, one of value, just like He gave them in the beginning.

Women today need to realize their worth and stand up for their rights.

Gen. 34:1-15

DINAH (judgment)

Dinah, born of Leah and Jacob,
Into the land one day fled,
For she was bored at home
And felt a need to roam.

What others did often see
Piqued Dinah's curiosity.
But, alas there was no escape,
So by a lad she was raped.

The lad then asked for her hand,
Pledged to open up the land
For both their nationalities
To share in all liberties.

But Dinah's brothers went wild
For their sister had been defiled.
They then devised a plan,
To kill all related to Shechem.

Father Jacob did lament,
For the disgrace brought unto him.
The important thing he forgot;
Sin is not again man - but God.

LESSONS FROM DINAH

Dinah was a young girl who lived in a time when female children were thought not to have much value.

She was given the job of minding the goats.

As she looked around at the girls who were not a part of the Israelite tribes, the grass surely must have appeared green.

But, like many of us, she soon learned that with freedom comes responsibility.

Dinah discovered that we are not islands unto ourselves and that our actions also affect the lives of others.

Because of one foolish whim, death and destruction came not only to Dinah and her family, but also to a whole other nation.

Temptation is always lurking about. We need to learn from Dinah to look before we leap; to think about the consequences of our actions. Life does not have to be a wild roller coaster of a ride for it to be exciting. It becomes boring when we focus on self. The best way to get a new perspective is to look beyond yourself. Perhaps if Dinah had been doing a really good job of minding her goats, she would have saved herself and others a lifetime of pain.

Perhaps if Dinah had paid heed to some of her family history she would have known better.

Both her grandfather and her great grandfather had compromised the virtue of their wives for self-gratification.

History teaches us many lessons.

We as women of today need to pay heed to history.

Gen. 39:1-20

POTIPHAR'S WIFE (fat bull's wife)

An Egyptian woman was she,
One with a lot of liberty
To go along with her wealth
And her obsession with self.

Too much time upon her hands
Seemed to increase her demands,
For her eyes began to roam
When her husband was not home.

She invited young Joseph in
For a night of sexual sin;
But, being strong, he refused,
Alas, she claimed to be abused.

So Joseph was dressed in prison garb;
Thrust into Potiphar's cell so dark.
But Joseph was not lost there
In spite of the wife of Potiphar.

'Tis her name that disappeared,
To ne'er be heard nor revered.
As Potiphar's wife she is known,
With no identity of her own.

LESSONS FROM POTIPHAR'S WIFE

Potiphar's wife had everything that money and position
could buy.

She was the wife of a high-ranking official in the Egyptian
government.

She was also given more freedom than most women
of her day.

But Potiphar's wife was discontent.

She never learned that situations do not bring
happiness nor peace.

Potiphar's wife felt dissatisfaction because her life
held no purpose.

Potiphar was away a good deal of the time on business
and this left Potiphar's wife with too much time on her
hands.

The old saying "an idle mind is the devil's workshop" is
certainly proven in her life.

Potiphar's wife centered her thoughts and actions on
what's in it for me. Then when she did not get her own way,
she sought revenge. It mattered little to her that she had to lie
in order to accomplish this revenge. Potiphar's wife had an
empty life because she tried to fill it up with things that are
not what God wants as priorities in our lives.

We as women need to look to God to find the purpose
for our lives.

If we are always looking into ourselves,
we can never see God.

To miss seeing God is not only a fate worse than death,
it is eternal death.

We also need to remember the importance of truth
in our daily walk.

There is always the temptation to tell just the
little white lie.

There is no such thing.

Even the smallest lie always comes home to roost,
much to our dismay.

God also admonishes us that vengeance belongs to Him.

WOMEN IN THE TIME OF TRANSITION

The Israelites had been in Egyptian captivity for over four hundred years.

They had suffered humiliation, persecution, and death at the hands of the Egyptians who had once offered food and land in the time of Joseph.

Now they cried out daily for deliverance.

God not only had heard their cries, but was preparing a way of deliverance and a deliverer.

The time period from this point until the time God gave the Israelites the Kings they demanded in the Promised land is filled with Heroic Women.

These women rose to the forefront during the deliverance from Egypt, through the forty years of wandering in the desert, to the trying times of overtaking and occupying the Promised land.

As we study them we will see one who was a prophet,

one who was a judge,

one of ill repute,

one who thought only of herself,

one who gave her son to God,

one who became bitter,

and one who would continue the line
to Jesus ancestry.

First let us look at the life of Miriam...

Ex. 2-15; Num. 12:20; Deut. 24-9; I Chr. 6:3; Micah 6:4

MIRIAM (exalted)

To have a brother big and bold
Can be difficult, I am told.
Especially you see —
When he is younger than thee.

This was Miriam's place
According to God's grace.
Moses would lead the band,
While she gave a helping hand.

Miriam held him as a child,
Then watched him in the Nile.
'Twas her responsibility
To see to Moses' safety.

A Prophetess she became,
Herald throughout the land,
As she spoke the words
God would give to her.

Then as Moses grew
He became God's tool.
Blinded by jealousy,
Miriam ask: "Why not me?"

To which God did reply
Yours is not to ask why.
God gave her leprosy,
A dreaded death decree.

But Moses intervened,
So God made her clean
From this one little slip
Of a very human lip.

So now when we think of her,
We see joy and we see mirth
As she sang and danced with glee
As they crossed the Red Sea.

LESSONS FROM MIRIAM

Miriam was the sister of two great men, Moses and Aaron.

But Miriam always felt that she was their equal because God had also given her a place of authority in His plan to redeem His people.

We can learn from Miriam that God can and does place women in places of authority, yes, even places of authority over men outside of marriage.

When God speaks to you and says to perform any task, you need to be obedient only to God.

Miriam also teaches us that one does not have to be married to be fulfilled or used by God.

Miriam may have never married although tradition says she was the wife of Hur, either way she had a very productive and obviously happy life.

She not only was a Prophet,

but also a songwriter

and a musician.

She did not let age become a barrier. She was 100 years old when the Israelites crossed the Red Sea and guess who was the first woman across? You got it, it was Miriam singing and dancing and playing her tambourine! God intends for us to be active and useful in His kingdom forever!

One warning we can glean from the life of Miriam is found in her attitude of jealously. We need to not concern ourselves about how and what God is doing in others lives and concentrate on what He has given us to do. God has equipped each of us with abilities to fit the task He has for us. We need to accept our individual places of service knowing that God chose them so they are a part of His perfect plan. He and He alone makes room for each of His children and the gifts He has given them.

We can also learn of God's mercy and His grace in His healing of Miriam. You too can be made whole!

Josh. 2; 6:22, 23; Matt. 1:5; Hebrews 11:31 and James 2:25

RAHAB (public place)

One time a long while ago,
'Twas in the city of Jericho.
There lived a woman called Rahab
Whose reputation was quite bad.

She lived along the city's wall.
Her house was open to one and all
For lodging and another use—
You see, Rahab was a prostitute.

When the Hebrew spies came
Fear filled up the land,
But courage filled her heart
For she believed in their God.

Rahab took in the spies,
Then told her people lies.
God's reward we can see
In how He saved her family.

God works often times
Thru folks we decline.
He looks far beneath
Our natures ever weak.

Into our deepest heart
To see if He has a part.
Then He gives us time
To get our lives in line.

Rahab's name is now renowned,
In the Hall of Faith she is found;
Recorded in the Hebrew book
Because of the stand she took.

LESSONS FROM RAHAB

Rahab was a prostitute who lived along the wall of the city of Jericho.

When the Israelites came to claim the Promised Land, they had to contend with this wall.

Joshua sent spies into the land to scope out the situation.

When these spies ran into trouble, Rahab took them into her home at the peril of her life and family.

When her people came looking for these spies, Rahab said they were not there and then lowered them over the wall in a basket.

Because Rahab believed in the God of Israel, she was not afraid to take action.

God rewarded her faithfulness by saving her family from destruction when the walls of Jericho fell.

God does not look on the outer shell,
but knows the heart full well.

We humans too often judge others by the circumstances of their lives. We put ourselves up as a yard stick by which to measure others worth. The real measuring tool is Jesus Christ. Next to Him none of us make the cut, but by His blood He and He alone raises our stature. He says to "judge not lest ye be judged."

We would have rejected Rahab because of her occupation, but God used her and blessed her life. He did not say: "Get your life in order that I may use you." He said: "I accept you where you are and I will set your life in order by my love."

We can learn from Rahab to trust God and
"take in the spies".

Then He will remove the danger and deliver His own.

Judges 4 & 5

DEBORAH (word)

There once was a woman named Deborah
Who allowed God to control and use her.
He made her a Judge of Israel
Who advised and planned quite well.

God filled her with confidence, insight,
And the knowledge to do what was right.
Not once did she seek for fame;
To serve God was her only aim.

Even on the battlefield,
She carried forth God's shield.
The enemy fled that day,
'Tho his chariot there did stay.

Her battle cry still holds true—
"Does not the Lord go out before you?"
Deborah's faith made her strong,
Helped her right many a wrong.

She was a woman and a wife
Yet she balanced out her life.
Which proves once again—
For all, God has a plan.

And when we yield our will to His,
He'll touch our lives with a kiss.
Our days will be filled with song
Because it is to God we belong.

Thus like Deborah of old
We can walk and be bold;
Sharing all of God's word
'Til all the lost have heard.

LESSONS FROM DEBORAH

Deborah was one of those women who had it all.
You know the ones we all envy.

She was a prophetess,
  poet,
    singer,
      wife,
        judge,
          patriot,
            military expert
and even had a royal palm tree growing in her yard!

Her fame came in the area of her wisdom and her guerilla warfare even though she was an excellent, loving wife - the perfect homemaker.

Deborah was given the powerful position of Judge in Israel.

She was the only woman to whom God gave this type of authority over both men and women.

Because Deborah followed God's instruction she was able to balance the seeming contradictory situations.

Deborah did not neglect her wifely duties and God made time for both.

She was the lady so many of us strive to be - homemaker and career woman.

Deborah used her insight and knowledge at God's direction. This gave her the confidence to serve knowing the decisions she made would be right. Deborah put her money where her mouth was, so to speak, by leading the troops into battle, encouraging them with the admonition "Does not the Lord go out before you" until the battle was won.

When Deborah received praise she directed it back to God because she knew where the credit belonged. We would do well to take a page out of her book! But Deborah's life had many pages - all worthy of emulation. The main lesson we can learn from Deborah is to only go where "The Lord has gone out before us." Being strong in faith in God while yielding to the Holy Spirit can make super women of us all. Super women who give the glory to God.

Judges 16

DELILAH (languishing)

In the Valley of Sorek,
Samson and Delilah met.
Her beauty caught his eye,
He would pay by and by.

For her heart was full of greed;
Of his love she had no need.
To gain the secret of his power,
Was to be her finest hour.

So she nagged and cajoled
Until ole Samson told
How the length of his hair
Gave him strength to spare.

Now she had him in her snare
So she cut off all his hair.
The Delilah felt no remorse
As Samson slipped off his course.

But her plan went awry;
Her people were to die.
As God shows once again
Don't mess with my man.

LESSONS FROM DELILAH

Delilah was a very beautiful woman.

A woman who knew how to use her beauty to get what she wanted.

She failed to recognize that outward beauty fades and that it is the inner beauty that radiates forever.

She lived in the time when Samson was Judge over Israel.

Samson was a mighty man because God had so gifted him.

Samson was also a weak man in that he could not curb his appetites.

Enemies of Israel recognized these qualities in both Samson and Delilah and decided to use their weaknesses to bring about the fall of Israel.

Although their plan backfired, we can learn a lesson in priorities from the experience of Delilah.

Priorities! Where are yours?

Delilah had hers in the wrong place.

Her "what's in it for me" attitude not only brought frustration and strife it eventually cost her life.

Money, possessions and position are not the things that bring true happiness.

Another bit of wisdom can be reaped from Delilah and that is the tragic consequences that occur when one uses another person.

Manipulation always backfires sooner or later.

Lies and hypocrisy are the tools of Satan.

When we use them we are in his workshop.

God says we cannot serve two masters - choose this day whom you will serve.

Ruth

NAOMI (agreeable)

Naomi had to leave her land,
Because there was a great famine.
She left the town of Bethlehem
With her sons and her husband.

Into the land of Moab they did go,
In the days of long ago.
They dwelt there nigh on ten years,
Then Naomi's eyes filled with tears.

'Twas time to speak the awful truth,
To both Orpah and sweet Ruth.
For Naomi had heard it said,
Back in Bethlehem there was bread.

This helped her to understand
The reason for the famine.
It had been a warning sent from God
About the ways His people trod.

Naomi knew now where she belonged,
She would confess to God her wrongs.
But, the daughters in her care
Would not be welcomed there.

'Tho she had shared with them her faith,
They would face prejudicial hate.
So thru tears and a heart that was rent,
She said: "Go back home to your parents!"

Naomi then would be all alone,
The thought chilled her to the bone.
But, her love, unselfish and true,
Knew "twas the only thing to do.

Orpah, though sad did go home.
But, Ruth stood firm like a stone.
"Whither thou goest, I will go,
Your people and God I will know."

So to the land of Judah they returned,
A great lesson Naomi had learned.
God's blessing or His curse,
Depend upon obedience to His words.

Then in her twilight years,
Naomi no longer wept bitter tears.
God had blessed her thru Ruth.
She saw a grandson's first tooth!

"Tho her blood flowed not in his veins,
The bond was there just the same
Sweet Ruth for Naomi had become
More precious than even seven sons.

Now Naomi had not one inkling,
This child would be a special link.
Little Obed was destined to be
The grandfather of a king!

Yes, and David would be his name
From his line the Savior came.
'Twould not be for a thousand years,
But, He would dry all Mother's tears!

LESSONS FROM NAOMI

Naomi was a God-fearing woman who put her family first.

While this is a good trait, it is in disobedience to God's command.

God says that He is to be first in our lives.

Naomi, like each of us, had to face the consequences of disobedience.

She found herself in a strange land grieving the loss of both of her sons, her husband and home.

Naomi used her head and the good sense God gave her and realized what she had to do to again receive God's blessing in her life.

But, this would mean sacrificing all that was left of her family, her daughters-in-law.

Because she loved them she made an unselfish decision that would be in their best interest.

Naomi's willingness to put God first and others ahead of herself rather than become bitter or wallow in self-pity was rewarded beyond her wildest imagination.

God secured her future and gave her a loving family in her native land.

If the old adage "a picture is worth a thousand words" is true, then we, as women today, would fare well to look into the face and heart of Naomi!

Hers is a life well worth modeling.

Ruth

RUTH (satisfied beauty)

"Whither thou goest I will go."
Words spoken by Ruth long ago
To the mother of the man,
She had once called husband.

Death had dealt its blow
Leaving grief here below.
But now because of love
Ruth moved on down the road.

To the land of Israel's God
Gleaning grain from the sod.
Until upon one night
Boaz took her for his wife.

From the children that she bore,
We now live forevermore.
Because from her line
Came the Savior Divine!

LESSONS FROM RUTH

Ruth is a wonderful example for today's women.

She shows us the power of love and shared experiences.

It was in the sharing of their grief and futures that the bond was sealed between Ruth and Naomi.

Women gain a special strength during times of adversity because of their ability to share.

Their joy is also magnified through sharing.

Ruth helps us to understand that the loss of a spouse need not be the end. It is a change point certainly, but we need to realize "it ain't over 'til it's over", God just send us in another direction. If we shut down then we close the door on God's possibilities.

Ruth allows us to see that there can be positive in-law relationships if we are giving and accepting of others.

We need to remember that while we are accepting the negative aspects of another, they are also having to live with our faults.

It is when we can accentuate the positive that the negative shrinks before our eyes.

God intended for the older women to instruct the younger women.

This can only be done when both women have receptive spirits.

1 Sam: 1 & 2

HANNAH (gracious)

Hannah felt quite sad
Because she had no lad.
So upon one day
These words she prayed.

"God—if you grant my plea-
I'll give him back to thee."
Then to her great joy
God gave her a baby boy.

Time went by and Hannah knew,
T'was time to her word to be true.
So to the temple she trod,
Offering her Samuel up to God.

Hannah was wise and sincere,
Knowing that our children so dear
Are, but gifts to us from God,
To nurture and guide by His rod.

Until it is time to let go
Of their lives ebb and flow.
Trusting them into His hand
Knowing this is His Holy Plan.

LESSONS FROM HANNAH

Hannah lived in a time when it was considered to be a curse from God if a woman was not married and able to bear children.

Hannah was a God-fearing woman who was married, but had no children.

This made her very sad because she longed for this special gift from God of children.

So she prayed to God asking Him to give her a son and in return when that child was old enough she would take him to the temple and give him back to God.

God granted her request and true to her word, Hannah gave this child back to God.

God, in turn, gave her more children because He knew that Hannah knew how to be a good mother.

Hannah teaches us how to be a good mother.

First, we ask God to grant us the privilege of nurturing His precious gift of children.

Second, we dedicate and give them back to God.

Third, we take them to the temple;

and fourth, we let them go.

Too often, mothers want to hang on to their children and attempt to control their lives. They try to live out the disappointments of their lives by living out their dreams through their children. This can never work. It is a situation rife with problems and unhappiness. Life is only good when it is lived inside of God's will.

Hannah shows us the peace that comes from trusting God.

I Sam. 1: 1-8

PENINIAH (pearl, precious stone)

Peniniah was wed to a man named Elkanah
Who also was wed to a woman called Hannah.
This posed a problem, don't you see —
For Peniniah was filled with jealousy.

She had borne Elkanah many sons,
While Hannah, 'til now had none.
Yet, it happened year after year,
Elkanah favored Hannah, his dear.

So when holidays would arrive,
Peniniah would make Hannah cry,
For she flaunted all her sons
To this childless woman.

Envy and bitterness soon filled her soul
As Satan took over all control —
There was no joy within her life,
It was full of hatred and strife.

This is ever the way
When from God we stray.
He can only fill a heart
That first bears His mark.

LESSONS FROM PENINAH

Peniniah lived in a time when, although it was against God's law, man's law permitted a man to have more than one wife.

Peniniah was the first to bear sons to her husband, but his love went to another wife, Hannah.

Jealousy reared its ugly head and life was miserable for the whole family.

This is ever the case when man goes against the laws of God.

Peniniah probably could not help the circumstances of her life, but she did have control over how she dealt with those circumstances.

When we allow circumstances to open the door to Satan and his devices, there is no more room for God in our hearts.

Envy, bitterness, jealousy, and hate are all sins to God.

He tells us in His word that we are to confess all our sins and then bring them and lay them at His feet.

That means letting go of them.

We are then to ask Him to remove these sins from our lives, believe that He has and then thank Him for His forgiveness. This is called walking in the Spirit. The Holy Spirit comes into our lives to guide and comfort us. If we have our hearts so full of sin, the Holy Spirit cannot come in and function as God planned. To be filled with the Spirit, we first have to empty the vessel of our heart so He can fill us. It's like when we wake up and discover that we are up to our necks in the alligators of sin, we need to empty the swamp. Then ask for the filling of the Spirit so that there is no room for Satan and his devices that separate us from God.

Book of Job

JOB'S WIFE (he that weeps)

Job's wife stood and watched one day,
As Satan took it all away—
Their home, cattle and the land
Were all destroyed by his hand.

When their children all had died
And boils covered up Job's side,
She spoke out in anger and pain;
Words she could not restrain.

"Curse God and die!" said she.
But "God is good!" said he.
For Job had a faith so true
In the Sovereign God he knew.

Job is remembered for his faith;
His wife, only for her hate.
What a sad thing to see
When both could've been free.

For faith in God above
Remembers His great love.
Then when ill winds blow,
The stronger one may grow.

LESSONS FROM JOB'S WIFE

Job was a very righteous man.

God had blessed him with great wealth, health and family.

Satan went to God and asked permission to test Job's faith.

God granted Satan's request to prove that He had not "put a hedge around Job".

Satan did his worst and yet Job's faith was not shaken.

Job's wife and friends did not share as strong a faith as Job.

With each new tragedy, Job's wife lost more and more of her faith.

She even went so far as to rail at Job about his God and then shouted the infamous words, "Curse God and die!"

We are told nothing more about Job's wife, but I wonder how she reacted when God restored four times over to Job after the time of testing.

Perhaps she said, "Thank goodness, that's over!"

Or maybe, "It's about time!"

She could have said, "It could not have gotten any worse!"

But hopefully she also grew stronger in her faith after witnessing the greatness and the grace of God. Satan is allowed to roam about in this world seeking whom he may devour, but those who belong to the King of Kings do not have to fear. We should read the book of Job over and over again to learn how to handle adversity. An even more effective thing to do would be to read a few pages out of our own lives. God is ever busy taking care of His own. Do we recognize His hand upon our lives? Do we offer up thanksgiving or are we also guilty of cursing God?

WOMEN IN THE PROMISED LAND

Once the Hebrews had secured the promised land,

    they demanded that God give them a king.

The fact that God was to be their King seemed to have slipped their minds as they mingled with pagan people.

    God granted their request.

This began a downhill slide until finally,

    amidst an era of political decline,

        the Hebrews became captives once again.

It was during this period that we see the gamut run from women of excellence and faith to the very most wicked.

Let us begin with David's first wife, Michal, daughter of King Saul.....

I Sam. 14; II Sam. 6; I Chr. 15:29

Michal (perfect)

There once was a young girl
Who seemed to have the world.
For her father was King Saul,
She lived within the palace wall.

When David caught her eye,
Michal began to sigh.
This King Saul observed,
So he gave David his word.

For lovely Michal's hand;
100 dead Philistines in the land,
But to King Saul's surprise,
The battle David survived.

Michal became David's wife,
Even helped to save his life.
But when David from Saul fled,
Many tears Michal shed.

Bitterness filled her heart,
Because she knew no part
Of David's special love
For his God up above.

Then, as is oft' the way —
Her love turned to hate.
A life that once held hope
Was left in darkness to grope.

LESSONS FROM MICHAL

Michal was the daughter of King Saul and the first wife of King David.

But she was filled with jealousy.

David loved his God more than he loved her.

This caused the softness of a heart filled with love to become hard and bitter.

It is always a wonder how those who seem to have it all, seem to never have enough.

Bitterness is a scourge propagated by Satan.

If he can get us to hang on to disappointments, tragedies, and failures he can keep us captive forever.

Yes, life sometimes hands us a raw deal and we cry out that life is not fair.

But, God has never said that it would be fair.

He even told us that it would be hard and full of disappointments.

That is why when He ascended to the Father He sent the Holy Spirit because He knew we would need a Comforter.

The most beautiful of women can become hard and ugly because they cling to bitterness as if it were their lifeline.

Learn from Michal that a heart filled with bitterness leaves you alone, while life goes on leaving you behind because you refuse to let go of bitterness.

Another lesson we can learn from Michal is to not be a clinging vine.

Allow those you love the freedom to be who they are and to serve God as He directs.

I Sam. 25; II Sam. 2; I Chr. 3:1

ABIGAIL (maker of joy)

Every now and again
There appears a special woman
Who, in spite of the hand she's dealt,
Can make her presence felt.

Such a one was Abigail
Whose story now we'll tell.
She had both beauty and brains,
Knowing what she could change.

Married to a lesser man,
Abigail developed a plan—
When he dropped the ball,
She would trouble forestall.

One day while in the field,
Her husband failed to kneel
To the wishes of a king;
Death this could bring.

But, Abigail took haste,
Not a moment did she waste.
The persuasion of her speech
Repaired the deadly breach.

When her first husband died,
David took her for his bride.
Abigail once again,
Stood by her man.

She helped him to see
How things were meant to be.
Significant in each life
By being a very good wife.

LESSONS FROM ABIGAIL

Abigail was married to a man who had no regard for her.

He drank to excess and was not a good steward of his possessions.

He often found himself in a fix, which his wife Abigail would make right.

Abigail never usurped her husband's authority, but worked behind the scenes picking up the pieces and smoothing the way.

She even went so far as to take the blame when David and his men were refused food.

Her husband had arrogantly refused to help David because as he put is, "Who is he to me?"

As the next in line to be King, David could have put him to death had not Abigail intervened.

Abigail was one of those women you look at and wonder how she got hooked up with a loser for a husband.

Abigail had beauty, brains, and a whole lot of common sense, not to mention a strong faith in God.

Abigail knew the advantage of speaking softly and choosing the right moment for action.

She teaches us the value of patience and loyalty.

From Abigail we also learn that God blesses a wife who points out the land mines to her husband and allows her to diffuse the explosive when she is wise enough to seek God's counsel.

We can also learn that when a woman is not self-seeking but seeking the best for others, God gives her life's best.

II Sam. 11 & 12; I Kings 1 & 2; Psm. 51.

BATHSHEBA (promise)

Bathsheba was caught between
Her husband and a king—
She had acted quite rash,
In choosing a site for a bath.

David should have been at war
But he was gazing from afar.
From these two wrongs we can see
How that night changed history.

Moments of weakness multiply
Quicker than a blinking eye.
Events went from bad to worse,
Sin chauffeured in a hearse.

Widowed, pregnant and afraid,
Rewards for vows betrayed.
'Tho she became David's wife,
Still things were not right.

That is until God intervened
Forgave and made them clean.
Blest their home with a son;
They called him Solomon.

Bathsheba now stood between
Her son and his Father king
And from their line would be
A Savior for you and for me.

LESSONS FROM BATHSHEBA

Bathsheba was married to a man named Uriah who was away serving in the army of King David.

Bathsheba was home taking a bath out in the courtyard of her home.

Mistake Number One.

David, who should have been at the front line with his soldiers, was standing looking out his window, which just happened to overlook Bathsheba's courtyard.

As is ever the case, an idle mind is the devil's workshop.

Tempted by the beauty of Bathsheba, David had her brought to him to be used for his pleaure.

Only one night, who would know?

God!

Bathsheba became pregnant and when she shared the news with David, he came up with a plan to deceive Uriah; but Uriah, being more faithful than David, would not go along.

David had another plan, which was to take the life of Uriah and then take Bathsheba for his wife.

But God—

will always reveal our sin.

Bathsheba soon learned that sins, no matter how small, are like small seeds that into mighty oaks do grow.

We are not pawns in the hands of others. How easy if would have been for Bathsheba to blame King David for her sin. After all he was the King. We have to recognize that we and we alone are responsible for our actions.

Remorse for our actions is essential to gain forgiveness and cleansing. Wrong actions and mistakes can be turned around by God, but we still have to ask for forgiveness and then live with the consequences. "The devil made me do it" is not a good excuse. The devil only has as much power as you and God allow him to have. If he is "making" you do something it is because you give him the authority over you. God gives us free will, but to not choose God is to choose Satan. There is no fence sitting in God's kingdom. God says, "If you are not with me you are against me." Beware your sins will find you out.

I Kings 16:31; II Kings 9:37

JEZEBEL (isle of the dunghill)

Jezebel, Jezebel, Jezebel,
A queen doomed to hell.
She was wicked , she was cruel,
She played Ahab for a fool.

Jezebel had great power,
T'was her hand that ruled the hour.
And the Northern Kingdom fell,
Because of her evil spell.

She was a thorn in Elijah's side,
For his God she could not abide.
The priests and gods that she knew
Had no power when day was through.

So as she lived, did she die,
One doesn't spit in God's eye.
T'was by the Jezreel walls,
She was eaten by the dogs.

Just as God had said on that day,
When He told the price they'd pay,
For following not after Him,
And leading Israel into sin.

LESSONS FROM JEZEBEL

Jezebel was woman who worshipped many gods, but self was her chief god.

She was in a position of power and influence which she used for two purposes.

First, her self-gratification

and second, her obsession of turning the Israelites against the one God they served.

Jezebel had a very hard and calloused heart.

When one has a hard heart it affects one's hearing. Jezebel could not "hear" the message from God that came from the prophet Elijah.

Today we live in a time when women are gaining more and more positions of power and influence. As women we need to make sure the sweet lotion of God's love is applied to our hearts so they remain soft and pliable enabling us to hear His message.

God commands that we put no other gods before Him, yet by placing family, jobs, possessions, self and etc. first in our lives we are doing just that.

Anything that displaces The True God is a god in our lives.

We can learn from Jezebel the folly and the danger that is inevitable when we do not give God first place.

Women should give God leadership over their lives and then use their influence to lead others to God not away from Him.

I Kings 17: 7-24

THE WIDOW OF ZAREPHATH
(ambush of the mouth)

One day as a widow was gathering sticks,
She thought her mind was playing tricks,
For a stranger had asked for bread,
As she was preparing for her death.

For in her house was no flour nor oil,
No matter how hard she might toil.
The stranger was a prophet of God,
Who held his head so very proud.

Perhaps she should just do,
The things he told her to.
For he said to "Fear not",
Because he spoke for God.

The widow did all that he said,
For many days making bread,
And never once did she find
That God treated her unkind.

Even when her son had died,
God her every need supplied.
For God answered Elijah's prayer;
Raised her son then and there.

What joy must have filled her soul
As she saw her son made whole.
Praise God! Now she knew,
Elijah's God was true!

LESSONS FROM THE WIDOW OF ZAREPHATH

The widow of Zarephath did not know about God.

She lived in a small town between Tyre and Sidon in Phoenicia.

She and her small son had only enough flour and oil to prepare a final meal before they died when she met up with the prophet Elijah at the city gate.

There had been a drought in the land and times were hard.

As the prophet asked help from her, she responded with her need.

But something in the voice of the prophet sparked a small seed of faith.

Acting upon this small seed of faith, the widow did as the prophet of God told her.

In acting in obedience she was rewarded with having her needs supplied daily.

It is very interesting to note that God did not supply her with a barrel of flour and a large bottle of oil, but only enough for each day's bread. What this says to me is that God rewards our faith, but only on a daily basis. We have to renew our faith every day. Our faith grows and we learn from experience that we can trust God's promises. As we learn to experience God, then He can bring us into a greater understanding of who He is. Faith is not a magic pill we take that lasts forever, but rather a step by step process.

We can learn, as did the Widow of Zarephath, that God not only takes care of the major events in our lives, but He is interested in all the little every day details.

The God that we can trust with our life is the same God that is interested in what we have for breakfast!

II Kings 5:1-5, 14, 15; Acts 1:8

A LITTLE JEWISH MAID

There once was a little Jewish maid,
Who had no choice where she stayed.
She now lived in Naaman's home
Doing chores from dusk to dawn.

But she knew this one truth,
God always looks out for you.
The goodness of His grace
Transcends both time and place.

A heart so full of God's love
Never drowns in the mud
Of life's circumstance.
It gives a second chance.

So when Naaman's destiny
Took him down with leprosy
The little maid spoke up
Heeding not the chance she took.

But Naaman heard her words
And to the river he did forge,
Where he dipped seven times
Leaving his leprosy behind.

Because of a young girl's faith,
Lives were changed on that day.
Naaman's home now knew
Only Israel's God was true.

LESSONS FROM THE LITTLE JEWISH MAID

The little Jewish maid was taken captive during a time of peace in Israel by a raiding band of troops of Syria's King Benhadad.

This could have made her very bitter and resentful, but this young girl knew the peace of trusting God regardless of life's circumstances.

Instead of hostility she exhibited love,

acceptance,

submission

and sympathy.

Because of this a family who did not know the only true God became believers.

Oh, if we could only learn the lesson of the little Jewish maid!

How much sorrow and wasted time could be adverted.

Truly she knew how to make lemon-aid when life hands you a lemon!

Two things are noteworthy about this young girl.

First, her lifestyle brought attention to her.

Second, she was not afraid to speak up about her God.

She did not preach a sermon nor espouse a lot of theology, all she said was what she knew - it was enough!

Don't let bitterness and resentment control your life.

When you do you only lose more of your life. We may not be able to control what happens to us, but we can control how we respond.

Our response should always be a childlike faith that relies upon God to make all things right.

II Chr. 34:22-23; 34: 1-21; 35: 1-19

HULDAH (the world)

"Thus saith the Lord!"
Yes, this was the word
Spoken again and again
By a prophetess in the land.

Now Huldah was her name;
To her many people came,
She gave advice from the Lord,
Striking anew a familiar chord.

She spoke out quite openly
In the court for all to see.
One day priests came to her
Seeking help with God's word.

They were sent by the King
Who was busy a worrying
About his people's sins,
And what God would do to them.

Huldah showed no fear,
Her answer was quite clear.
A message filled with doom
And future things to come.

She also spoke of grace,
So they cleansed the place
Of all the false idols
And had a great revival.

LESSONS FROM HULDAH

Huldah was a prophetess to the Israelites in a time when they had rejected God.

There were also two very prominent male prophets during this time,

Jeremiah and Zephaniah.

Huldah was married to the man who was in charge of King Josiah's wardrobe.

This placed her in a special position to be both a faithful wife and serve God.

God ever places us where He has prepared harts to hear if we will but be faithful and obedient to His commands.

God pens up the opportunities; we are to seize the moment.

Huldah practiced being obedient to her calling as a prophetess openly.

She was not ashamed to say, "Thus saith the Lord".

How we need this same attitude and courage today.

We sometimes go along to get along until the world cannot see any difference between believers and non-believers.

Because of Huldah's faithfulness, God used her to bring a nation back into His fold.

King Josiah's priests had found the word of God as they were repairing the temple. They had read that word to the king, but all were confused as to exactly what God's law meant. They were frightened because they knew that had not kept God's law.

Huldah could have said, "Go and ask Jeremiah or Zephaniah."

She could have said, "I'm not sure."

But Huldah did know and she knew that it was her responsibility to share what she knew to be from God. This is also our responsibility as women today. We need to share God's truths as He reveals them to us.

Could it be that because Huldah's life was orderly and not cluttered with unnecessary things, she was able to hear God when He spoke to her?

ESTHER

ESTHER (good fortune)

Long ago in a Persian land,
Xerxes took Esther's hand.
He was drawn to her smile
And her heart void of guile.

The beauty of her face;
That special kind of grace,
Made her the perfect one
To share a king's throne.

Yet, in her heart she knew
To her own God was due
Her loyalty and her trust
For He alone is just.

Esther's people were in need,
She made plans carefully,
For she and she alone
Had access to a throne.

'Tho she feared for her life,
She trusted God on one night.
Esther asked that others pray
While she tried a king to sway.

But, God had gone on ahead
To the man she had wed.
He often works behind the scene
To grant our fondest dream.

So things turned out all right
Death became Haman's plight.
Once again God had proved,
He will watch over you.

LESSONS FROM ESTHER

Esther was a young Jewish girl living in the land of Persia.

The king of Persia sent out a decree requiring all the eligible young women to present themselves to him so that he could select a wife.

Mordecai, who was Esther's uncle, encouraged Esther to present herself to the king, but to keep the fact that she was of Jewish descent a secret.

Esther presented herself to the king and was the one chosen to be his wife.

Later, when the king had learned to love Esther, she shared with him her Jewish heritage.

When the Jews' position in the land of Persia came into peril, God used Esther and her position as queen to deliver His people.

Esther's beauty was famous throughout the land, but to her credit, she seemed to know that outward beauty is a fleeting thing. Esther knew that her security did not rest in her looks or her position. She knew that God provides the only real security.

God gave Ester wisdom, sound judgment, self-control, courage, intellect and insight because she was devout, dedicated to her people, believed in prayer, had a sincere faith, was loyal and prudent

The lesson we learn from Esther is the importance of acting on our knowledge of God.

God has a purpose for each of our lives, which cannot be accomplished unless we choose to yield our will to His and obey His commands.

This becomes easy as we trust His promises, pray, work within His plan and experience His grace.

Like Esther, we can trust God in whatever situation He places us.

Our willingness to act for others, even to our own peril, can be a powerful witness to the security we feel as believers in the one and only Sovereign God.

WOMEN IN THE TIME OF JESUS

There had now been 400 years with no word from God. His prophets had all been rejected and God had let His people feel the emptiness of life without hope.

Then with the birth of John the Baptist,

God prepared His people for the ultimate deliverer,

His Son, Jesus Christ,

Who would, once and for all,

redeem those who would receive Him.

The women during the time of Christ show forth the strength that comes from having a

personal relationship with Jesus

and the total despair of rejecting Him.

Could we begin anywhere else, but with Mary, the Mother of Jesus?

All Four Gospels and Acts

MARY, THE MOTHER OF JESUS (exalted)

Mary, Mother of Jesus of Nazareth,
At His birth and at His death,
Was just an ordinary girl
Caught in an extraordinary whirl.

Going about life in her usual way,
God spoke to her upon one day.
When apprised of what was to be,
Her heart accepted the mystery.

To carry the Son of God
Was a most important job.
It held both joy and pain
As God's plan became plain.

Mary did all that God said,
'Tho she pondered in her head,
How this Son borne to me
Will set all men free.

Free, forever from sin's fee
To live with God thru eternity.
No wonder her heart burst with song,
Jesus would right every wrong.

The trials along the way
Would be worth it someday.
Available to God, Mary would be.
What about you and me?

LESSONS FROM MARY MOTHER OF JESUS

Mary was in her early teens when God chose her for the most extraordinary task ever to be performed by a woman on earth.

She was to be the mother of the Son of God.

Mary's life teaches us many lessons.

First, God can use us from the time of our birth until our earthly death.
We do not have to be a certain age.

Second, God chooses more often than not to use the ordinary people as they go about their ordinary lives.

In doing this, God can be sure that it is He who gets the glory.
As women we do not need to be concerned about what we can do, but rather our concern should center on being available as instruments for God's use.

The third lesson for us in Mary's life is to accept God's plan for our lives by faith.

We do not need to have all the answers in order to be used of Him.
Indeed, we probably would not understand the answers if we had them.
This is not to imply that we are not intelligent beings, but rather that the natural man does not understand God's ways and even our spiritual being will not understand all things until we see Jesus face to face in Heaven.

The fourth truth we can learn from Mary is to wait
upon the Lord.

Just as she pondered all things in her heart, that is what
we should do so that as He reveals His will we will recognize
His presence in the daily events of our lives. Mary went from
being a young eager bride to being pregnant out of wedlock;
from being the mother of the Son of God to being a single
mom; from the empty nest syndrome to the grieving mother;
from the heartbreak of blended family strife to the joy of a
Son brought up from the grave.

Undoubtedly, Mary had many questions along the way.
Yet, she trusted God and tried to be all that He wanted her
to be regardless of the circumstances of her life. It is our
response to the varied circumstances of our lives that reveal
our true relationship to God. It is all right to ask if you are
then content with having to sometimes wait upon the answer
until God's timing says you are ready to handle the answers.
A sound knowledge of God's word which is found in scripture and applied to our lives gives us the strength, just as it
did Mary, to take everything and lay it at the feet of Jesus.
Then we can trust that He will handle all things because He
is and will always be the One who is in control. He and He
alone has won the victory over Satan and death.

Luke 1: 5-20

ELIZABETH (the fullness of God)

Elizabeth, the mother of John,
Had a lot to think upon—
For she was advanced in years
When God's words she did hear

Thru Zacharias her spouse,
Who was a priest in God's house.
He told of the birth of their son
Whose name was to be called John.

For he would be great
When he entered the gate
To tell all lost men,
"Repent of your sins!"

When Mary came unexpectedly,
Elizabeth was filled with glee.
"O The Mother of my Lord!"
Were Elizabeth's first words.

For the spirit had shown her
All that was to occur—
As these two special sons
Redemption's work had begun.

LESSONS FROM ELIZABETH

Elizabeth was the wife of a priest.

This meant that she was a woman whose character was blameless.

We know this because all priest's wives had to be of high moral character so as to not defile their husband's ministry.

Elizabeth was also from the tribe of Aaron and was the cousin of Mary, the mother of Jesus.

Elizabeth was honored by God for her personal relationship to Him.

God gave her a special son late in life.

He instructed her husband concerning the child.

God knew that He could depend upon this couple to be faithful to His commands.

What an epitaph!

From the life of Elizabeth we can learn how faithful is God in His dealings with His children! Because Elizabeth was true to her God, she lived in peace and contentment regardless of being childless. God rewarded her with a son. God knows our every desire and need. In His time and in His way He will take care of everything in our lives. If we could but learn to trust Him as Elizabeth did, what a calm would reign over our lives.

God, not only gave Elizabeth a son, but He allowed her to know of the impending birth of His son, the Savior of the World.

She was the first to be aware of His presence.

God will also give the faithful today a special insight as to what He is doing and will be doing in the future.

The choice is ours to make:

will we be faithful and obedient to His commands or will we do as we please?

Jer. 49: 11; Psm. 147:3; Luke 2:22-27, 36-38

ANNA (gracious)

As Anna looked back o'er the years,
She saw no need for bitter tears.
The God she loved so dear
Had taught her not to fear.

Seven years of wedded bliss,
Were cut short by Death's kiss.
And though there was no heir,
Anna refused to despair.

She turned instead to God,
To His Temple she swiftly trod;
Making it her new home
Waiting for the Christ to come.

Yes, for over sixty years,
Anna prophesied here,
Then when the great day came,
Anna did His name proclaim!

God had allowed this faithful one
To see His only begotten Son.
The greatest moment of all age,
Was witnessed by this wise sage.

LESSONS FROM ANNA

Anna was widowed early in her marriage.
She could have sat down and let society take care of her and drowned herself in a sea of self-pity.

Anna did not do this; instead she gave her life to God.

In doing so, Anna obtained the peace that only
God can give.

In fact, God had a reward awaiting Anna that she could never have imagined.

For over sixty years she worked in the temple and prayed for the Messiah to come.

She told others daily that He was on His way.

But when God does not act as swiftly as we would have Him to sometimes we wonder if the truths of His word will occur during our lifetime on earth.

Just imagine the surprised old lady that day in the temple when Mary and Joseph brought the baby Jesus into the temple, as was required by law, and she recognized Him to be that long awaited Messiah!

Still Anna did not push and shove, but rather allowed the prophet Simeon to greet the young couple and proclaim that truly this was the Savior of the World!

Can you even start to comprehend how hard it must have been for Anna to keep silent.

Anna was content to look over Simeon's shoulder as he held the king of Kings!

From Anna we can learn the valuable lesson of patience
and faith.

Anna accepted that when God closes a door He opens up
a window of opportunity.

Our task is to be available.

We cannot be available if our eyes are blurred with tears
of grief and self pity.

We need to grieve for a season then dry our eyes and turn
them upward to heaven so we can see the way that God has
planned.

Luke 10:38-42; John 11:17-45

MARTHA (who becomes bitter)

Martha, who lived in Bethany
Had a lot of priorities
Which she felt quite sure
Other ought to endure.

Her siblings, Lazarus and Mary
Often found her quite contrary,
As she bustled all about
Taking care of the house.

For the welcome of her home
Was so very well known
That Martha often felt tense
From entertaining all of her friends.

When Jesus came to sup.
'Twas Martha that filled His cup.
While Mary sat around
Where Jesus feet were ground.

This made Martha feel distress.
As she tried to clean the mess.
So she murmured angry words
Which her Master surely heard.

He admonished Martha on that day
That Mary's was the better way
For 'tis only at the Masters' feet
One learns to live complete.

Later on when Lazarus died,
And others mourned and Mary cried,
Martha rush out into the street,
Jesus Christ to go and meet.

With disappointment on her face
Martha felt her Lord's embrace.
But her hope was there renewed
When she saw what Jesus would do.

He brought Lazarus back to life
Ending the four days of strife.
So when next He came to dine,
Martha served in silence this time.

For the lesson she had learned,
Was for Jesus Christ to yearn;
To get your priorities straight
While you His return await.

LESSONS FROM MARTHA

Martha was well respected in her community because of her industrious nature, her hospitality and her attention to detail.

Martha would also be well respected in any of our communities today for the same reasons.

We have a saying that goes something like this; "If you want something done, ask the busiest person you know."

But, like Martha, we need to learn that getting caught up in details and busyness can make us forget the main reason for our actions.

Service is good, but there is a proper time to listen and learn from Jesus and a proper time to serve Him.

Too often we get caught up in doing and going and we don't have time to develop a personal relationship to Jesus Christ. Church attendance and service are good, but it is the personal relationship with Jesus that makes us a child of the King.

Martha also teaches us that we cannot force our priorities upon others whether it be our work ethic or our salvation.

Each individual has to make the decision for themselves as to how and if they will relate to the Savior of the world.

It is faith in Jesus and knowledge that He is our hope in all situations that sustains us in both times of joy and adversity.

It is our calm in the midst of the storms of life that are our greatest witness as to our faith in the Almighty God, not our frantic actions.

A third lesson we can learn from Martha is not to look around and compare ourselves and our situations to others.

Each one of us has a unique place of service.

It is He who enables us.

We should not be concerned with the recognition of men, but rather be content in the knowledge that we have been faithful to the tasks that God has set before us.

Matthew 26:6-1;, Mark 14:3-9; Luke 10:38-42;
John 11:17-45; 12:1-11

MARY, LAZARUS SISTER (exalted)

Mary sat at Jesus feet,
Quiet, demure and discreet.
Eager to hear and to learn,
Menial tasks she spurned.

When this brought a sister's ire,
Jesus quickly put out the fire
With words meant to show,
Time was short here below.

Mary seemed the first to comprehend
Just how things were going to end.
Her knowledge became replete
From sitting at the Master's feet.

So when Jesus came again,
Mary had prepared a plan.
No longer content to sit,
'Twas time to do her bit.

As Jesus next sat down to dine,
Mary took action this time.
With costly perfume and her hair,
She washed His feet then and there.

'Twas then that Jesus knew
Mary knew what He was to do.
So He commended her deed
Forever in the world's memory.

LESSONS FROM MARY SISTER OF LAZARUS

Mary is our prime example of the importance of being still and listening for the still small voice of God.

Today we can hear His voice in His Holy Word, through others that He has ordained to speak, through the thoughts He puts into our minds and hearts as we worship Him and by being ever aware of what God is doing all around us.

If we would pay as close attention to Jesus as Mary we would see that He is present in all the events of our lives.

He is guiding us,

comforting us,

chastening us

and loving us.

If we cannot feel His presence then perhaps it is because we are too busy attempting to "run" our own lives.

We need to remember that we our not our own, but rather we belong to Him because He bought us with a price.

Like Mary we need to learn when to listen and when to act.

We also need to realize that it is not the size of the action, but the obedience that is important to God.

He can take the smallest act and give it widespread effect.

Our primary act of obedience should be to worship and praise His Holy Name.

Mark 6: 17-28

HERODIAS (glory of the skin)

Herodias wanted John's head
For the words he had said.
Hate and revenge took control
Then murder became her goal.

John had spoken out one day
On the sins she had displayed.
"It is not lawful", said he
"For you Herod's wife to be."

She used her daughter to gain
The head of this righteous man
Whose words were extolled
In hopes of rescuing her soul.

And 'tho blood stained her hand,
Repentance was God's demand.
The sin to her eternal grief
Was the fatal one of unbelief.

LESSONS FROM HERODIAS

Herodias was married to a man named Phillip who was the brother of King Herod Antipas.

Herod, although he was also married to another, decided that he wanted Herodias for his wife.

Both Herod and Herodias then left their original partners in order to live together.

Because Herod was king no one dared to say anything except John the Baptist.

John confronted them with their sin and showed them a way of repentance.

Herod was proud and egotistical and self-serving.

Herodias shared these characteristics plus a mean spirit.

Instead of repentance and sorrow for their sin the couple continued to live together.

Meanwhile, Herodias was filled with hate and the desire for revenge.

When her daughter was dancing before the king and gained his favor, Herodias seized upon the opportunity to rid herself of John the Baptist.

She instructed her daughter to ask the king for John's head on a platter.

Although he was not as keen on the idea as Herodias, Herod granted Salome's request.

Guilt, hatred, pride and self are like poison in our souls.

When we allow these emotions to control our thinking we do radical things, which have fatal consequences.

The natural man is inclined to yield to these feelings, but when we are in Christ Jesus we become a new creature. One whoever strives to be like Jesus.

God's laws do not change.

We live in a time when society accepts many things outside of God's law. We need to remember that as children of God we are not of this world and therefore should not live according to the mores of the world.

When we sin, we should be quick to repent and ask God for forgiveness.

John 8:1-7

THE ADULTEROUS WOMAN

The adulterous woman was caught one nite
In bed with yet one more man.
The whole scene was a frightful site
As the crowd bond up her hands.

They dragged her down the street,
Shouting and crying out loud,
How she had been so indiscreet
To the ever increasing crowd.

At the feet of Jesus she was thrown;
She dared not look into His face;
As others her sins made known,
Great was the woman's disgrace.

Then Jesus did a curious thing,
He stopped and drew upon the sand.
And there amongst the whisperings
Jesus stood and brushed off His hand.

"Let him who is without sin
Be the first to cast a stone."
As these words came from Him
The accusers headed for their home.

Jesus asked a question of her
To which she did reply,
"They are all gone, Sir"
And she uttered a heavy sigh.

"If they find no fault, "He said,
"Neither then do I."
Then as He gently lift her head,
With relief she began to cry.

" Go, now and sin no more"
Were Jesus words to her.
She now was free to open the Door
As the spirit in her began to stir.

LESSONS FROM THE ADULTEROUS WOMAN

To be an adulterous woman in the days of Jesus was a crime punishable by death.

But on this particular night, the angry crowd was not as interested in justice as they were interested in trapping Jesus.

Jesus simply pointed out the obvious to the crowd.

Since mankind fell in the Garden of Eden, there seems to be an inherent need to see other peoples sin as worse than our own.

Certainly, adultery was and is a sin, but was it worse for the woman than the men with whom she was involved?

Sin is anything that separates us from God, and there is only one unforgivable sin with God.

That sin is the sin of unbelief in His Son Jesus Christ.

The adulterous woman learned on that night that there is nothing that God will not forgive in us if we display a contrite heart.

But once we are forgiven we are to "Go and sin no more."

Now this does not mean that we will live exemplary lives, but rather that we will always be striving to be like Jesus.

When we fail, we must go and confess our sin and He will give us a new awareness of the forgiveness that He purchased for each of us on Calvary's tree.

To hang on to feelings of guilt, is to say that God is not capable to pardon our sins.

We can also learn from this story that we need to be concerned with seeking forgiveness for our own sins, rather than busy pointing out the mistakes of others.

> We are to point others to Christ, not point out
> their sins to Him.

He already knows all about each of us. We should pray for one another rather than condemn.

Could we not also learn just to wait upon the Lord?

John 4: 4-26

THE WOMAN AT THE WELL

The hour was late, 'twas time to go,
So off she went on down the road
To draw some water from the well
Before the darkness of night fell.

What was that by the well?
Was it a man? She couldn't tell;
But as she then drew near,
Her heart was filled with fear.

For a man did sit there;
She would best be aware.
As she drew water, she looked down,
To avoid yet one more frown.

But then He spoke to her
Asking for a drink of water.
When she asked Him, "Why?
This was His reply:

"If you, but only knew
Who asks a drink from you,
You would ask and receive
The Living Water free."

Then as they conversed,
He looked deep into her.
As she received His truth,
Back to town she fairly flew;

To bring all who dwelt there
Back to the well where
They too could drink up
Life giving Water from His cup.

LESSONS FROM THE WOMAN AT THE WELL

The woman at the well was a Samaritan.

She had lived a rather colorful life.

She had been married at least five times and was now living with a man to whom she was not married.

Her life style made her unpopular with the ladies of the town.

To avoid their whispers and disapproving stares, she went to the well for water when she thought no one would be there.

She was surprised to find a Jewish man there who had no problem talking with her.

This Jewish man was Jesus, and He is always available when we want to talk with Him.

As they talked, she realized who Jesus was referring to when He talked of the Living Water.

As soon as she knew the Truth, she forgot all about the town and their unforgiving spirit.

All she could think of was bringing them to Jesus.

Have you had a little talk with Jesus lately?

Jesus still sits and talks with us if we have a personal relationship with Him.

He talks to us in His Holy word, the Bible,

He talks to us through other believers

He talks to us through the Holy Spirit that dwells in each believer,

and He talks to us through circumstances.

God always confirms that He is talking to us when He speaks to us in ways other than the Bible. We need to become aware of what God is saying so that we, like the woman at the well, can forget about our past, be filled with a forgiving spirit bringing others to Him.

Eugenia Price says in her book "The Unique World of Women", God is no respecter of persons, but He is a respecter of every heart.

Matt. 27,28; Mark 15, 16; Luke 8:2, 23, 24; John 19,20

MARY MAGDALENE (exalted)

Mary Magdalene, we are told,
Followed Jesus brave and bold,
After He had cleansed her life
Of seven demons causing strife.

'Twas a thankful heart
That gave the start
Of this faithful friend
Whose love knew no end.

The freedom Christ gave to her
Kept her strong and made her sure
As she traveled day by day,
Walking down the narrow way.

She stood and watched that day
As they took Jesus life away.
But her joy was renewed
When Jesus tomb she viewed.

For she had gone at break of day
Her last respects there to pay.
But she found He was not dead
He spoke words of love instead.

What an honor to be the one
First to see God's risen Son.
Mary then knew what to do,
She went and shared the good news.

LESSONS FROM MARY MAGDALENE

Mary Magdalene loved Jesus with all of her heart.
From the moment He cast out the demons in her life she turned her life over to Jesus.

She traveled with Him;

she ministered to Him

and to the other disciples.

She contributed to the needs of the group financially.

She was always there.

If anyone deserved the title of disciple it was Mary, but Mary Magdalene was not interested in titles or position, she was interested in serving her Lord because out of a thankful heart came much love.

What an example for us as women today!

Mary Magdalene's life also teaches us that women were and are still vital to the ministry of Jesus. Although we live in a society that would have us believe otherwise Jesus recognized and used women extensively.

Jesus relates to women as equal reflectors of God's image.

But perhaps the most valuable lesson we can learn from Mary Magdalene is that when we are obedient, we grow in understanding.

Then as we grow in understanding we are given more tasks
to perform for God's glory.

It is interesting to note that the reward for service
is more service.

Our only motive for service should be an overwhelming
love for the God who sent His Son to die for us because He
first love us.

WOMEN OF THE NEW TESTAMENT CHURCH

Jesus Christ has now been crucified for the sins of mankind,

He has been buried in the tomb

and then raised on the third day

and has ascended to His Father.

The victory over sin and death has been won.

He has told his disciples to go to Jerusalem and to wait.

He will send the Holy Spirit.

When the Holy Spirit fell upon those who were waiting, the New Testament Church had it's beginning; for Peter began to preach and the lost were reached.

Women in the New Testament Church show us the amazing strength God gives us through His Holy Spirit which now dwells in all believers.

God has given unto all who believe, not only salvation, but spiritual gifts which enable us to be His hands, His feet, His eyes, His mouth, His ears, His ambassadors, His missionaries.

The only women of the New Testament Church who failed were those who obviously did not have a personal relationship with Jesus, but rather, a superficial faith.

These women are beautiful examples of what we as women in the modern church should be all about.

Acts 4:32; 5:11

SAPPHIRA (beautiful)

Sapphira, in Jerusalem dwelt,
Each day in the temple she knelt
Along with her husband and her friends,
As together their lives they blend.

One for all and all for one;
First allegiance to God's Son
Was the creed of this sect,
Each gave all with no regret,

Except for Sapphira and her man.
They developed an alternate plan.
From the property they sold
A portion they did withhold.

When ask why they had lied,
Both fell down and died.
Not from deceiving other men,
Lying to God was their sin.

All that glitters is not gold,
We learn from this tale of old.
Forever they lost the chance
Before God's throne to dance.

A difference Sapphira could've made
Before those sad fateful days
By giving all of her love
To our Lord God up above.

But she chose the lesser way
And by her death she did pay.
No treasure here upon this earth
Is greater than the "New Birth".

LESSONS FROM SAPPHIRA

Sapphira was the wife of a man named Ananias.

Together they had joined up with a group of people whose goal was to follow Christ and care for others.

This group of people, known as Christians, had been filled with the Holy Spirit ten days after Jesus had ascended into heaven.

They met daily in the temple to pray and worship God.

The leaders of the group such as Barnabas felt a leading of the Spirit to sell all their worldly goods and put the yield into a mutual fund for everyone in the group to share.

Sapphira and Ananias wanted to fit into the group, so they sold some property and pretended to give all of the profit to the church.

Peter, sensing that they had withheld a portion, questioned them individually concerning their gift.

Both Ananias and Sapphira lied.

God struck them both dead, not for withholding a portion of the profit, but for the hypocrisy of their gift and the lie to God.

God loves a cheerful giver, but His stomach is turned by lukewarm offerings.

This has nothing to do with the size of the gift, but rather the spirit in which it is given.

God does not need our gifts, He wants our love.

We need to examine our reasons for giving to God.

Do we give because it is expected, or because we want to impress men?

We may fool some of the people some of the time, but we can never fool the God of the Universe.

The greatest gift we can give to Him is a heart fully yielded to His will.

Belonging to a group or a church is not enough, one must have a personal relationship with Jesus in order for their natures to be changed enough to give it all.

Acts 9:36-42; Romans 12:4-8; James 1:27

DORCAS (the female of the roe-buck)

Dorcas was an "old maid"
Joppa is where she stayed;
With no thought of herself,
She gave others her help.

A needle and a thread
Helped her earn her bread.
But 'twas more than a job,
It's how she served her God.

For to Dorcas don't you see
Everyone was her family.
Busy from morn 'til night,
She helped ease their plight.

But one day she fell ill,
Then death stayed her skill;
Until Peter came along
And silenced Death's song.

The first thing Dorcas said
"Hey! "I'll get the bread,
All of these hungry ones
Need each and every crumb."

For you see life to her
Was a chance to serve
Both others and her God
According to His Holy Word.

131

LESSONS FROM DORCAS

Dorcas was an unmarried woman in a time when it was not a popular thing to be, yet she did not sit home and feel left out of the mainstream of life.

She didn't nurse the loneliness that so often accompanies a single household.

Dorcas did not feel her worth depended upon being married.

Dorcas got up and about, busy and involved in the life of her community and others.

The result was she not only was a useful member of society, but loved by all who knew her.

Dorcas knew Jesus Christ as her personal Redeemer and is the only woman in scripture that is called a disciple of Jesus.

This tells us that she was active in sharing the good news of Jesus.

Her life is a witness even today all over the world.

She is the only woman scripture records as being one of seven persons who was raised from the dead

It is only as we are willing to lay down our life that Jesus can raise us up to new life in Him.

We can learn from Dorcas that our worth is not measured in our marital status, but rather in whose we are.

Because she was so full of the love of God it overflowed in her life.

As she brought happiness and joy to others it was returned multiplied to her.

Acts 16:11-15, 40

LYDIA

One day by a riverside,
Came a woman from Thyatira.
Now a seller of purple was she,
A business woman you see.

Lydia, as she was called,
Was also a worshipper of God.
She stopped and heard Paul's words,
Her heart was opened by the Lord.

She was baptized then and there
At this special place of prayer.
As she arose from her knees,
Lydia issued this plea-

"If I have been faithful in any way,
Won't you come to my house to stay."
And so that's how it all began,
Her sharing Christ with all men.

No longer in business for herself,
Now with God she shared Her wealth.
For he became her first priority
Held up high for all to see.

LESSONS FROM LYDIA

Lydia was the CEO,

 the president,

  the business manager

   and the sales force

    in a very lucrative business.

This must have been a time consuming responsibility, yet, Lydia took time out in her day for God.

Scripture records that she was gathered with some other women in the middle of the day at what the Apostle Paul thought was a special place of prayer.

We know that Lydia believed in God, but she did not have the saving grace of Jesus Christ until Paul shared that with her on that day.

What a difference it made in her life!

She still was a businesswoman, but now she used her business acumen to bring others to God.

She responded to God with action.

This truly is a praise song to God!

Since there was no temple in her community, Lydia opened up her home. She took in the needy, the hungry, and the outcasts of society and together they worshipped God in her home. Sure she had bad hair days, but Lydia did not let that keep her from being about the Master's business first and foremost. But, like all saints, she sometimes needed encouragement and she was not ashamed to take it from others. We read where when Paul and others were released from prison they went first to Lydia's house and OFFERED ENCOURAGEMENT! The best way to reach the lost for Jesus is to make friends of them first, and the best way to make friends is to let them help YOU! We all like to be the one offering aid, but sometimes it is difficult for us to admit need. Admitting need levels the ground that lies between potential friends.

Acts 18: 1-4, 18-20, 24-26; Romans 16: 3-5; I Cor. 16:19

PRISCILLA (ancient)

Priscilla went throughout the land,
Making tents with her man
And everywhere that they stopped
They shared the news about their God.

They met up with Paul one day
And because they had the same trade,
He went with them to stay
As he preached along the way.

Later, in the city of Ephesus,
They heard Apollos discuss
All the ways of the Lord
At least, what he had heard.

But he knew only about John,
So they taught him further on,
Explaining very carefully
So he would preach accurately.

Faithful to God where'er they went,
That's how their lives were spent.
These fellow-workers of Paul
Knew how to give it all.

LESSONS FROM PRISCILLA

Priscilla and Aquilla were forced to leave their home and travel about because of political circumstances.

They made the best of a bad deal.

One might wonder what might have been if they had not been in the right spot at the right moment to be a friend to the Apostle Paul.

Paul asks others to give thanks for Priscilla and Aquilla because if it were not for them he would not have his life.

We need to learn from Priscilla that wherever God has you, that is the place He wants you to serve Him for that moment.

What may seem to us to be an adverse circumstance could be the Divine plan of our Heavenly Father.

Where ever you are you need to be busy sharing what you know about Jesus Christ.

Discernment is also something that Priscilla and Aquilla practiced.

When they heard others speak about the Word of God they listened very closely.

When they found facts lacking they had the courage to speak up even though the person speaking might be more gifted speaker, more renowned in the land, or higher up on the education ladder.

This is also what God commands us to do today.

He says that in the last days there will be many false prophets and teachers.

It is our job to know the truth and ferret out false or inadequate teachings when we hear them.

We can only do this if we know what God's word says.

This comes from studying His word and being open to the Holy Spirit's revelations.

We also learn from Priscilla and Aquilla the importance of helping and encouraging other saints.

Romans 16: 1-2

PHOEBE (shining, pure)

Who was this woman Paul called sister?
Why look! Her feet are all blistered!
Why has she come so far alone,
Many a mile away from home?

Paul says to treat her like a saint
She came because Paul can't
To tell us how Christ died
Our salvation to supply.

Phoebe, yes, that's her name
Because of her nothing is the same.
She had told Paul she would try,
For none are as unhindered as I.

Phoebe's journey was far and hard
One that would have made men tired.
She led the way down through the age
For us to have the Roman page.

The Roman page of words so true
Of all Christ has done for you.
Can we do any less today
To show others "His Way"?

LESSONS FROM PHOEBE

Phoebe was an unmarried woman who obviously devoted her singleness to do God's work.

She knew that because she was unencumbered with the responsibilities of a family she was able to do more for her lord.

She did not have to consult anyone for permission to serve when and where ever.

Because Phoebe had this freedom lifestyle, she was available to take the gospel message to the Romans.

Paul had never been able to take the message of Jesus Christ to Rome and was not able to go for three more years.

Who knows how many came to know Jesus in that three-year period because Phoebe dared to do the unusual.

As women today we don't need to shy away from a task God places before us just because it has never been done that way before. We need to be open to God's direction and available to go where He leads us.

Phoebe's services were many, they were sacrificial and they were effective.

With a faith like Phoebe yours can be too!

Paul called Phoebe sister—a kinship we all share who knows Christ as Savior, God as Father

There is a lesson for us in that one word.

What a difference we could see everywhere we are if we would love all of our "sisters".

Too often, we suffer from the "Cinderella Syndrome" in our relationships with other women.

I I Tim. 1: 5; 3: 14-17; Acts 16: 1-3

LOIS (better)

A grandmother was she
To a man called Timothy.
Now Lystra was their home
Where God was always welcome.

So, along with Timothy's mom
Lois helped to carry on,
Instructing this grandson
Concerning God, the Holy One.

A grandmother with enough time
To tell of the Lord Divine,
Ah, but even better still
To live according to His will.

In her Timothy could see
All God desired him to be.
She helped a grandson to know
Him from whom all blessings flow.

LESSONS FROM LOIS

Lois was a widowed grandmother who lived in the home of her daughter.

She could have felt sorry for herself and spent her days complaining, but she knew that God was not through with her yet.

Lois knew that there was still lots of work to do and that all she had to do was look around and get busy.

Grandmothers are very special.

They have the time, experience, and patience to give careful instruction and the grace to listen.

Young Timothy probably had a million questions and Lois was there to listen and answer those questions.

Lois also was a very wise mother.

She knew when to step in and help and when to step aside and allow her daughter to lead her son.

This is a very special trait that we as grandmothers sometime forget.

We get too eager to get the job done the way we know or feel is the correct way.

We need to remember that as progress continues, there are sometimes better ways than we know.

We are not told that Lois prayed specifically, but I know that if she was as close to the Lord as scripture implies, she was a prayer warrior.

Prayer is the best gift we can give to our children and grandchildren.

Just to bring them before God's throne and
leave them there.

There is not enough that can be said about the influence a
Godly grandmother can have upon a young life. To see faith
in action over a long period of time is a great witness to the
faithfulness of God. As others watch you go through all the
trials and joys of life continually at peace, then they can see
God through you.

I I Tim. 1:5; 3: 14-17; Acts 16: 1-3

EUNICE (Good Victory)

A Jewish woman named Eunice,
Whose faith was not diminished,
'Tho married to a Greek
Who did not the Lord seek.

Together they had a son
Treasured in their home.
'Twas there his mother shared
About how the Lord cared.

Their son grew to be a man
Who figured in God's plan;
For he traveled with Paul
Sharing God's word with all.

All of this might not have been
Had not his mother given him
Instructions from the Lord
And training in His word.

The many hours spent
With ears carefully bent
While at his mother's knee
Helped him hear the Spirit's plea.

For Eunice did not say
We'll let him go his own way.
She knew it was her place
To tell him of God's grace.

LESSONS FROM EUNICE

Eunice lived in Lystra and was a part of a faithful group of Christians.

Paul speaks of her as a fellow worker with him in the spreading of the gospel.

It seems that she gave Paul and others a lot of encouragement, but the greatest gift she gave them and God was her son, Timothy.

She was able to give this gift because she trained her son to love and serve God so that when the opportunity came he was ready.

Paul calls Timothy his "son in the faith".

Eunice was one of those women that many of us can identify with today.

She was a believer in Jesus as the only begotten Son of God and her Savior, but was married to a man who was not only not a believer, but also of a different nationality.

Life could not have been easy in her home.

Many women would be tempted to say, "We'll just raise him "neutrally" and let him make his own mind up later. He is young and I don't want to influence him."

Isn't that a scary statement, and yet many of us by our actions have made that statement.

We are going to influence our children whether we plan to or not.

We need to use that influence to bring them to the saving grace of Jesus Christ.

Once that has been accomplished it is our duty to train them up in the admonition of the Lord so that they may serve Him and trust Him as they live each day.

This is the greatest gift we can give to our children.

It gives them the courage to face each day because they will have the hope of tomorrow.

Romans 16:13

RUFUS'S MOTHER

On the Via Delarosa
As Jesus stumbled there,
Simon moved a little closer
Christ's cross to ably bear.

What did he see upon Christ face
That forever changed his life?
Perhaps 'twas the look of grace
As he later told his wife

For Simon's life did change.
We know that from his son
Who often helped to arrange
The work Paul had begun.

One mention of Rufus's name
'Twas in a letter from Paul.
His only claim to fame
He had answered God's call.

Paul, his Christian brother
As they toiled for their Lord,
Said they shared a mother
It is written in God's word.

But how could this be—?
For Rufus and the Apostle Paul
Were not from the same family tree,
As apples are said to fall.

Well, might it just be
When Paul felt all alone
This mother saw his need
And opened up her home?

Paul felt no need to explain
As he often did with others.
Paul only made this claim,
He called her his "Mother".

She touched him with a glove
Too soft for the world to see.
She gave him a mother's love
Whenever there was a need.

" Can we do any less?" asks God,
"In service or in prayer,
Than to do this simple task;
When needed—Just be there.

For this is a mother's place,
And should be our prayer;
"By His love and by His grace,
Yes, Lord- I'll be there!"

LESSONS FROM RUFUS'S MOTHER

There is nothing more precious, except the love of God, than a mother's love.

Everyone should know this love, but this is not always the case.

We do not know what happened to Paul's biological family, perhaps when he met Jesus on the Damascus road and gave his life to God, his family disowned him.

We do know that no mention of Paul's biological family is found in scripture.

Paul, like all of us, had times when he needed this unconditional type of love that mothers can give.

There must have been times when he needed a place to rest,

a home cooked meal,

the warmth of a fire,

the unconditional acceptance,

the listening ear.

It appears that Rufus's mother gave this to him.

Paul mentioned Rufus's mother in the Roman letter, but he did not mention her name. This was deviating from his usual pattern. Paul usually mentioned a person's relation to him or the church when he mentioned their name, but not with Rufus's mother.

Could it be that Paul felt like the people to whom he was writing would know the name of this woman who was so adept at this mother love business?

Regardless, Paul called her by the most beautiful name on earth, My Mother.

Surely when God made the female part of mankind, this was a primary task He intended for us to do.

To love those who needed love whenever there was a need.

To just be there.

I I Timothy 2: 20-21

In a wealthy home there are dishes made of gold and silver

as well as some made from wood and clay.

The expensive dishes are used for guests,

and the cheap ones are used in the kitchen or to put
garbage in.

If you accept the righteousness that Jesus Christ offers
you by His grace you will be like one of these dishes made
of purest gold-

the very best in the house-

so that Christ Himself can use you for His highest purposes.

ALPHABETICAL LISTING OF NAMED WOMEN IN THE BIBLE

Abi- I I Kings 18:2- Daughter of Zechariah, wife of Ahaz
and mother of Hezekiah, King of Judah
Abiah- I Chron. 2:24- Wife of Hezron
Abigail I- I Sam. 25:3, 14, 18, 23, 32, 36, 39, 40, 42
27:3
30:5
I I Sam 2:2
3:3
I Chron. 3:1- Widow of Nabal, wife of David
Abigail I I – I I Sam. 17:25; I Chron. 2:16, 17- Sister of
David
Abihail I- I Chron. 2:29- Wife of Abishur
Abihail I I – I I Chron. 11:18- Daughter of Eliab, wife of
Rehoboam
Abijah- I I Chron. 29:1- same as Abi
Abishag – I Kings 1:3, 15; 2:17, 21, 22-Maid from the town
of Shunem
Abital – I I Sam. 3:4; I Chron. 3:3- Wife of David
Achsah- Josh 15:16, 17; Judg. 1:12, 13; I Chron. 2:49-
Daughter of Caleb
Adah I – Gen. 4:19, 20, 23- Wife of Lamech
Adah I I – Gen. 36:2, 4, 10, 12, 16-Wife of Esau
Agar- Gal. 4:24- 25- Sarah's Handmaid

Ahinoam I- I Sam. 14:50- Wife of Saul
Ahinoam I I – I Sam. 25:43; 27:3; 30:5; I I Sam. 2:2; 3:2;
 I Chron. 3:1- Wife of David
Ahlai – I Chron. 2:31-Daughter of Sheshan
Aholah – Ezek. 23:4, 5, 36, 44-Symbolic name for Samaria
Aholibah- Ezek. 23:4, 11, 22, 36, 44-Whore in Ezekiel's
 allegory
Aholibamah – Gen. 36:2, 5, 14, 18, 25-Wife of Esau
Anah – Gen. 36:2, 14, 18, 25-Daughter of Zibeon
Anna – Luke 2:36-38-First Woman to Acclaim Christ
Apphia – Philemon 1:2-Christian of Colossae
Asenath – Gen. 41:45, 50; 46:20-Wife of Joseph
Atarah – I Chron. 2:26-Second wife of Jerahmeel
Athaliah – I I Kings 8:26, 11:1, 2, 3, 13, 14, 20-Daughter
 of Jezebel and Ahab, only ruling Queen of Judah I I
 Chron. 22:2, 10, 11, 12; 23:12, 13, 21; 24:7
Azubah I – I Chron. 2:18, 19-First wife of Caleb
Azubah I I – I Kings 22:42, I I Chron. 20:31-Daughter of
 Shilhi, wife of King Asa

Baara – I Chron. 8:8-Wife of Shaharaim
Bashemath I – Gen 26:34-Daughter of Elon, first wife of
 Esau
Bashemath I I – Gen 36:3, 4, 10, 13, 17-Second wife of
 Esau
Basmath – I Kings 4:15-Daughter of Solomon
Bathsheba – I I Sam. 11:3; 12:24; I Kings 1:11, 15, 16, 28, 31;
 I Kings 2:13, 18, 19; I Chron. 3:5-Wife of
 David and mother of Solomon
Bathshua – I Chron. 3:5-same as Bathsheba
Bernice – Acts 25:13, 23; 26:30-Sister of Agrippa I I
Bilhah – Gen. 29:29; 30:3,4,5,7; 35:22, 25; 37:2; 46:25; I
 Chron. 7:13- Rachel's handmaid, mother of Dan and
 Naphtali, grandmother of Samson through Jacob

Bithiah – I Chron. 4:18-Daughter of one of the Pharaohs, who married mered, descendant of Judah

Candace – Acts 8:27-a hereditary appellation used in the same manner as was the term Pharaoh, ruled in Ethiopia in the time of Paul

Chloe – I Cor. 1:11-a Corinthian woman in the time of Paul

Claudia – I I Tim. 4:21- A woman in the Christian Church at Rome

Cozbi- Num. 25:15, 18-a Midianitish woman slain at Shittim by Phinehas, son of Eleazar and grandson of Aaron

Damaris – Acts 17:34-A woman of Athens, who believed in the message of Paul.

Deborah I – Gen. 35:8-Rebekah's nurse

Deborah I I Judg. 4:4, 5, 9, 10, 14; 5:1, 7, 12, 15- judge and prophetess

Delilah – Judg. 16:4, 6, 10, 12, 13, 18-The Philistine woman who lured Samson

Dinah – Gen. 30:21; 34:1, 3, 5, 13, 25, 26; 46:15-Daughter of Leah and Jacob

Dorcas – Acts 9:36, 39-Woman Peter raised from the dead

Drusilla – Acts 24:24-Wife of Felix, Roman procurator at Caecarea

Eglah – I I Sam. 3:5; I Chron. 3:3-One of David's eight wives

Elisabeth – Luke 1:5, 7, 13, 24, 36, 40, 41, 57-Mother of John the Baptist, cousin of Mary, Mother of Jesus

Elisheba – Exod. 6:23-Wife of Aaron

Ephah – I Chron. 2:46-Concubine of Caleb

Ephratah – I Chron. 2:50; 4:4-Same as Ephrath

Esphrath – I Chron. 2:19-Mother of Hur and Wife of Caleb

Esther – Esther – a Jewess, who became the wife of
     Ahasuerus, king of Persia
Eunice- I I Tim. 1:5-Daughter of Lois, mother of Timothy
Euodias – Phil. 4:2-Deaconess in the church at Philippi
Eve – Gen. 3:20; 4:1; I I Cor. 11:3, I Tim. 2:13-the first
     woman, wife of Adam, mother of Cain, Abel, Seth.

Gomer – Hos. 1:3-Wife or concubine of Hosea

Hadassah – Esther 2:7-Hebrew name of Esther
Hagar – Gen. 16:1, 3, 4, 8, 15, 16; 21:9, 14, 17; 25:12-
     Sarah's Egyptian handmaid, mother of Ishmael
Haggith – I I Sam. 3:4; I Knigs 1:5, 11; 2:13; I Chron. 3:2-
     Fifth wife of David and mother of Adonijah
Hammoleketh – I Chron. 7:18-Mother of Ishod, Abiezer
     and Mahalah
Hamutal – I I Kings 25:31; 24:18; Jer. 52:1-Daughter of
     Jeremiah
Hannah – I Sam. 1:2, 5, 8, 9, 13, 15, 19, 20, 22; 2:1, 21-
     mother of Samuel
Hazelelponi – I Chron. 4:3-Woman in genealogies of Judah
Helah – I Chron. 4:5, 7-One of two wives of Ashur
Heph-zibah – I I Kings 21:1-Wife of King Hezekiah.
     Mother of Manasseh
Herodias – Matt. 14:3, 6; Mark 6:17, 19, 22; Luke 3:19-
     wife of Herod
Hodesh – I Chron. 8:9-Wife of Shaharaim
Hodiah – I Chron. 4:19-Same as Jehudijah
Hoglah – Num. 26:33; 27:1; 36:11; Josh. 17:3-One of
     Zelophehad's five daughters
Huldah – I I Kings 23:14; I I Chron. 34:22-Prophetess
Hushim – I Chron. 8:8, 11-One of the two wives of
     Shaharaim
Iscah – Gen. 11:29-daughter of Abraham's younger brother
     Haran, sister of Lot and Milcah

Jael – Judg. 4:17, 18, 21, 22; 5:6, 24-wife of the Kenite
　　Heber
Jecholiah – I I Kings 15:2, I I Chron. 26:3-wife of Amaziah
Jedidah – II Kings 22:1-Mother of Josiah, daughter of
　　Adaiah, wife of Amon
Jehoaddan – II Kings 14:2; I I Chron. 25:1-wife of Joash
Jehosheba – II Kings 11:2-daughter of King Jehoram
Jehudijah – I Chron. 4:18-genealogical name
Jemima – Job 42:14-the eldest of Job's three daughters
Jerioth – I Chron. 2:18-wife or concubine of Caleb
Jerusha – II Kings 15:33; I I Chron. 27:1-queen mother,
　　daughter of Zadok, wife of Uzziah, mother of
　　Jotham
Jezebel I – I Kings 16:31 18:4, 13, 19; 19:1, 2; 21:5, 7, 11,
　　14, 15, 23, 25
　　　　II Kings 9:7, 10, 22, 30, 36, 37-daughter of the
　　　　king of the Zidonians, wife of Ahab
Jezebel II – Rev. 2:20-symbolic name
Joanna – Luke 8:3; 24:10-wife of Chuza
Jochebed – Exod. 6:20; Num. 26:59-mother of Moses,
　　Miriam and Aaron
Judah – Jer. 3:7, 8, 10-an allegorical reference to the
　　country of Judah
Judith – Gen. 26:34-daughter of Beeri, Hittite wife of Esau
Julia – Rom. 16:15-Early Christian woman in Rome

Keren-Happuch – Job 42:14-Job's third daughter
Keturah – Gen. 25:1, 4; I Chron. 1:32, 33-second wife of
　　Abraham
Kezia – Job 42:14-second daughter of Job

Leah – sister of Rachel, wife of Jacob Gen. 29:16, 17, 23,
　　24, 25, 30, 31, 32; 30:9, 10, 11, 13, 14, 16, 17, 18,
　　19, 20; 31:4, 14, 23; 33:1, 2, 7; 34:1; 35:23, 26;
　　46:15, 18; 49:31; Ruth 4:11

Lois – II Tim. 1:5-Grandmother of Timothy, mother of
     Eunice
Lo-ruhamah – Hos. 1:6, 8-daughter of Gomer
Lydia – Acts 16:14, 40-Businesswoman of Philippi, first
     Christian convert in Europe

Maacah – Same as Maabhah
Maachah I – Gen. 22:24-Daughter of Abraham's brother
     Nahor
Maachah II – II Sam. 3:3; I Chron. 3:2-daughter of Talmai,
     one of David's eight wives, mother of Absalom
Maachah III – I Kings 15:2; II Chron. 11:20, 21, 22-
     daughter or granddaughter of Absalom
Maachah IV – I Kings 15:10, 13; II Chron. 15:16-mother of
     Asa
Maachah V – I Chron. 2:48-one of Caleb's concubines
Maachan VI – I Chron. 7:15, 16-wife of Machir, mother of
     Peresh and Sheresh
Maachah VII – I Chron. 8:29; 9:35-wife of Hehiel
Mahalah – I Chron. 7:18-daughter of Hammoleketh
Mahalath I – Gen. 28:9-wife of Esau
Mahalath II – II Chron. 11:18-grandaughter of David
Mahlah – Num. 26:33; 27:1; 36:11; Josh. 17:3-One of five
     daughters of Zelophehad
Mara – Ruth 1:20-Same as Naomi
Martha – Luke 10:38, 40, 41; John 11:1, 5, 19, 20, 21, 24,
     30, 39; 12:2-Sister of Lazarus and Mary of Bethany
Mary I – Matt. 1:16, 18, 20; 2:11; 13:55; Mark 6:3; Luke
     1:27, 30, 34, 38, 39, 41, 56; 2:5, 16,
19, 34; Acts 1:14-Mother of Jesus
Mary Magdalene II – Matt. 27:56, 61; 28:1; Mark 15:40,
     47; 16:1, 9 Luke 8:2, 24:10; John
19:25; 20:1, 11, 16, 18-first to report to the disciples the
     resurrection

Mary of Bethany III – Luke 10:39, 42; John 11:1, 2, 19, 20, 28, 31, 32, 45; 12:3; Mark 14:3-9-sister of Martha and Lazarus

Mary IV – Matt. 27:56, 61; 28:1; Mark 15:40, 47; 16:1; Luke 24:10-wife of Cleophas, mother of James and Joses John 19:25

Mary V – Acts 12:2-mother of John Mark

Mary VI – Rom. 16:6-woman singled out by Paul as a fellow laborer at Rome

Matred – Gen.36:39; I Chron. 1:50-Mother-in-law of Hadar

Mehetabel – Gen. 36:39; I Chron. 1:50-daughter of Matred, wife of Hadar

Merab – I Sam. 14:49; 18:17, 19-King Saul's eldest daughter

Meshullemeth – II Kings 21:19-wife of Manasseh, mother of Amon

Michaiah – II Chron. 13:2-Same as Maachah 3

Michal – I Sam. 14:49; 18:20, 27, 28; 19:11, 12, 13, 17; 25:44-daughter of King Saul, David's first wife II Sam. 3:13, 14; 6:16, 20, 21, 23; 21:8; I Chron. 15:29

Milcah I – Gen. 11:29; 22:20, 23; 24:15, 24, 47-daughter of Haran, wife of Nahor

Milcah II – Num. 26:33; 27:1; 36:11; Josh. 17:3-one of five of Zelophehad's daughters

Miriam I – Exod. 15:20, 21; Num. 12:1, 4, 5, 10, 15; 20:1; 26:59 Deut. 24:9; I Chron. 6:3;

Mic. 6:4-sister of Moses and Aaron, daughter of Jochebed

Miriam II – I Chron. 4:17-daughter of Ezra

Naamah I – Gen. 4:22-first daughter mentioned in Bible

Naamah II – I Kings 14:21, 31; II Chron. 12:13-wife of Solomon, mother of Rehoboam

Naarah – I Chron. 4:5, 6-wife of Ashur

Naomi – Ruth 1:2, 3, 8, 11, 19, 20, 21, 22; 2:1, 2, 6, 20, 22; 3:1; 4:3, 5, 9, 14, 16, 17-wife of Elimelech, mother of Mahlon and Chilion, mother-in-law of Oprah and Ruth

Nehushta – II Kings 24:8-daughter-in-law of King, daughter of Ellnathan

Noadiah – Neh. 6:14-false prophetess

Noah – Num. 26:33; 27:1; 36:11; Josh. 17:3-one of the five daughters of Zelophehad

Oholibamah – Same as Aholibamah

Oprah – Ruth 1:4, 14-sister-in-law of Ruth, wife of Chilion

Peninnah – I Sam. 1:2, 4-one of two wives of Elkanah

Persis – Rom. 16:12-woman in the early Roman Church

Phanuel – Luke 2:36-Asherite mother of Anna

Phebe – Rom. 16:1-2-deaconess in church at Cenchrea

Prisca – Same as Priscilla

Priscilla – Acts 18:2, 18, 26; Rom 16:3; I Cor. 16:19; II Tim.-wife of Aquilla, helper of Paul 4:19

Puah – Exod. 1:15-midwife in the time of Moses

Rachel – Gen. 29:6, 9, 10, 11, 12, 16, 17, 18, 20, 25, 28, 29, 30, 31; 30:1, 2, 6, 7, 8, 14, 15, 22, 25; 31:4, 14, 19, 32, 33, 34; 33:1, 2, 7; 35:16, 19, 20, 24, 25: 46:19, 22, 25; 48:7; Ruth 4:11; I Sam. 10:2; Jer. 31:15; Matt. 2:18-wife of Jacob, sister of Leah

Rahab I – Josh. 2:1, 3; 6:17; 23, 25; Heb. 11:31; Jas. 2:25-harlot who aided Israel spied

Rahab II – Matt. 1:5-wife of Salmon, mother of Boaz

Rebekah – Gen. 22:23; 24:15, 29, 30, 45, 51, 53, 58, 59, 60, 61, 64, 67; 25:20, 21, 28; 2;6:7, 8, 35; 27:5, 6, 11, 15, 42, 46; 28:5; 29:12; 35:8, 49:31; Rom. 9:10-wife of Isaac, mother of Jaco and Esau

Reumah – Gen. 22:24-concubine of Abraham's brother
    Nahor
Rhoda – Acts 12:13-maidservant in Jerusalem house of
    Mary, mother of Mark
Rizpah – II Sam. 3:7; 21:8, 10, 11-concubine of Saul
Ruth – Ruth 1:4, 14, 16, 22; 2:2, 8, 21, 22; m3:9; 4:5, 10,
    13; Matt. 1:5-moabite daughter-in-law of Naomi,
    wife of Mahlon and Boaz

Salome I – Matt. 20:20; 27:56; Mark 16:1-8-wife of
    Zebedee, mother of James and John
Salome II – Herodias daughter; Not actually named in the
    Bible, Josephus called Herodia's daughter Salome.
Sapphira – Acts 5:1-wife of Ananias
Sarah I – Gen. 11:29, 30, 31; 12:5, 11, 17; 16:1, 2, 3, 5, 6,
    8; 17:15, 17, 19, 21; 18:6, 9, 10, 11, 12, 13, 14, 15;
    20:2, 14, 16, 18; 21:1, 2, 3, 6, 7, 9, 12; 23:1, 2, 19;
    24:36, 67; 25:10, 12; 49:31; Isa. 51:2, Rom. 4:19;
    9:9; Heb. 11:11; I Peter 3:6-wife of Abraham and
    mother of Isaac
Sarah II – Gen. 46:17; Num. 26:46; I Chron. 7:30-daughter
    of Asher and Granddaughter of Jacob and Leah
Sarai – same as Sarah I
Serah – Same as Sarah II Gen. 46:17, I Chron. 7:30
Shelomith I – Leb. 24:11-daughter of Dibri of the tribe of
    Dan
Shelomith II – I Chron. 3:19; Matt. 1:12; Luke 3:27-
    daughter of Zerubbabel
Shelomith III – II Chron. 11:20-daughter of Maachah and
    King Rehoboam
Sherah – I Chron. 7:24-daughter of Beriah
Shimmeath – II Kings 12:21; II Chron. 24:26-Ammonite
    mother of Jozachar
Shimrith – II Chron. 24:26, same as Shomer
Shiphrah – Exod. 1:15-midwife in time of Moses

Shomer – II Kings 12:21-Moabite mother of Jehozabad

Shua – I Chron. 7:32-daughter of Heber

Susanna – Luke 8:3-one who ministered to Jesus of her substance

Syntyche – Phil. 4:2-member of the early Church at Philippi

Tabitha – same as Dorcas

Tahpenes – I Kings 11:19, 20-Queen of Pharaoh of Egypt in time of David

Tamar I – Gen. 38:6, 11, 13, 24; Ruth 3:12; I Chron. 2:4-mother of Pharez

Tamar II – II Sam. 13:1, 2, 4, 5, 6, 7, 8, 10, 19, 20, 22, 32; I Chron. 3:9-daughter of David and Maacah, sister of Absalom

Tamar III – II Sam. 14:27-daughter of Absalom

Taphath – I Kings 4:11-one of the daughters of Solomon

Thamar – Matt. 1:3 same as Tamar I

Timna – Gen 36:12-concubine of Esau's son Eliphaz, mother of Amalek

Tirzah – Num 26:33; 27:1; 36:11; Josh. 17:3-one of five daughters of Zelophehad

Tryphena – Rom. 16:12-early worker in the church at Rome

Vashti – Esther 1:9, 11, 12, 15, 16, 17, 19; 2:1, 4, 17-wife of Ahasuerus

Zebudah – II Kings 23:36-mother of Jehoiakim

Zeresh – Ester 5:10, 14; 6:13-wife of Haman

Zeruah – I Kings 11:26-widow woman, mother of Jeroboam

Zeruiah – I Sam. 26:6; II Sam. 2:13, 18; 3:39; 8:16; 14:1; 16:9, 10; 17:25; 18:2; 19:21, 22; 21:17; 23:18, 37; I Kings 1:7; 2:5, 22; I Chron. 2:16; 11:6, 39; 18:12,

15; 26:28; 27:24-Half sister of David, sister of
Abigail II

Zibiah – II Kings 12:1; II Chron. 24:1-wife of Ahaziah,
mother of Jehoash

Zillah – Gen. 4:19, 22, 23-one of two wives of Lamech

Zilpah – Gen 29:24; 30:9, 10; 35:26; 37:2; 46:18-Leah's
handmaid, mother of Gad and Asher

Zipporah – Exod. 2:21; 4:25; 18:2-daughter of Jethro, wife
of Moses, mother of twin sons

Printed in the United States
61671LVS00002B/28-33

9 781600 345197